GEORGE HERBERT MEAD

Essays on His Social Philosophy

GEORGE HERBERT MEAD
Essays on His Social Philosophy

Edited, with an introduction by
JOHN W. PETRAS

TEACHERS COLLEGE PRESS
Teachers College, Columbia University
New York

Foreword

A S PHILOSOPHER AND PSYCHOLOGIST, George Herbert Mead was a master of creativity and innovation. Although this statement will come as no surprise to those who are familiar with his writings, the fact remains that very little of the entire scope of his work has been widely available. Mead's reputation as a social psychologist was firmly established with the appearance of *Mind, Self, and Society* in 1934.[1] Other works that command less attention within the behavioral sciences have provided readers with some indication of his philosophy and its relationship to his social psychology, which he labeled *social behaviorism*.[2] The articles that have been selected for this volume reflect three aspects of Mead's work that have remained relatively unappreciated throughout the years. Many of these essays appeared before his social psychology became known in any systematic published form. Therefore, they are of special interest and value to the reader who has even a limited acquaintance with the theoretical foundations of Mead's interactionist psychology. Those who are familiar with the writings of John Dewey cannot help but be impressed by the degree of mutual influence that existed between these two friends while they were colleagues at the University of Chicago.

The first eight essays reflect Mead's early interest in the status of education in this country. Many of the ideas that run through these early articles are easily interpreted within the larger scope of his social psychology. In his statement on "The Editorial Policy of the *Elementary School Teacher*," Mead poses the primary problem of education as that of tempering the natural spontaneity of the child with the larger controlling influence of the community. Whereas the child's own impulses provide the source for his motivation and attention, this innate tendency must be fashioned by an intelligently constructed social environment in order to assure functional socialization into the community. The child's sense of spontaneity or play and its role in the educational system had been discussed by Mead in his article, "The Relation of Play to Education," which appeared in 1896. Essentially, this article calls for the establishment of an educational system that would be cognizant of the nature of self-development in the child. There is no problem of instilling motivation in the child; there is, however, a problem of creating a social atmosphere that will allow the child's own motivations to be channellized in a manner that is both socially and individually functional. The recognition that the child reacts in his environment as a social self led Mead to emphasize the importance of the *social* situation of the classroom. The relationship between motivation, spontaneity, and the situation form the subject matter of "The Psychology of Social Consciousness Implied in Instruction."

Aside from the problems of education that relate to the particular learning experience of the child, Mead also concerned himself with the broader problem of the social relationship existing between the school and the rest of society. Mead saw the creation of an effective learning environment within the school as dependent upon the situation outside of the school. The meaningfulness of the school depended upon the meaningfulness of the situations encountered by the child in his daily activities. There appears to be little doubt that Mead's personal involvement in the educational system of Chicago had considerable influence upon his educational theory. With 43 per cent of the children in the Chicago school system never completing an elementary education, Mead had launched an attack upon the curriculum of the schools. The course of study had traditionally been tailored to fit the needs of the middle-class student. As a partial solution to this problem he urged the incorporation of vocational education and trade schools into the elementary school network. In calling for the development of a trade school system as part of the public school system, Mead expressed the hope that this would enable these schools to remain within the hands of a voting public rather than a particular interest group, for example, manufacturers. This was the message that he brought to organized labor in an attempt to achieve its support for such a system.

The organic nature of society and the functional relationship between its parts was stressed by Mead as the framework for the establishment of a successful organization of parents. Such an association, Mead noted in "The Basis for A Parent's Association," must rest upon the foundation of a shared social existence. In turn, this social unity between the home and the school is related to the school's success or failure in exercising moral control over the child. It becomes imperative, therefore, to deal with the school and its functions within the context of the entire social order. Only in this manner does morality have experienced meaning for the child.

Mead's theory of ethics is synonymous with that of Dewey, resulting in the characteristic attack upon absolutism and traditionalism. The nature of the moral control that is exercised over the child by the school can be generalized to the nature of the moral control that is exercised by society over its members. Thus, morality must be infused with meaning. The individual cannot be reached with abstract ideals in the governing of his behavior, but, in Mead's words, ". . . by an ethics that is simply the development of the intelligence implicit in his act." Mead's ethical theory, then, is strongly rooted in his view of human nature as elaborated in his social psychology. Man and society are co-determinants. In both cases, the social situation provides the "raw material" for the act, which is then related to the individual's behavior through his interpretation of meaning. It is the nature of man to act in society as a social self. The psychology that had attempted to identify human nature as something inherent within the individual was expressed in an ethical theory that ignored the relationship between man and his social environment. Mead points out that one of the consequences of this approach was the lack of any attempt to reach the individual through his social situation. The *conditions* for the individual's behavior remained unaltered. In "Philanthropy from the Point of View of Ethics" and "The Psychology of Punitive Justice," Mead concerns himself with the important role of social conditions in providing a framework for the particular manifestations of certain natural inclinations in man.

The methodology of social reform receives a word of caution from Mead in "The Working Hypothesis in Social Reform." Here he addresses the problem of social planning in a society which is already characterized by a rapid rate of social change. The article affords us with an excellent example of how Mead conceives the relationship between society and reflective intelligence in man.

The idea that the development of the social nature of the individual results in the widening scope of what he internalizes as a "generalized other" provides the theme for the concluding essay, "The Psychological Bases of Internationalism." The reformer is seen as the man who must remove himself from the restrictions of nationalism and speak with a voice for all humanity.

These articles, then, serve to demonstrate the interrelatedness between Mead's social behaviorism and more particular aspects of his thought. In this sense, the ideas they contain are as pertinent today as they were at the time of their original publication.

This foreword and the introduction following have profited from the critical remarks and suggestions of Floyd Dotson, Jerold Heiss, Walter Wardwell, and, most of all, Joseph Zygmunt. Special thanks are due Herbert Blumer, who took the time to comment upon the introduction in its unrevised form.

JOHN W. PETRAS

Notes to the Foreword

1. Charles W. Morris (ed., Chicago: University of Chicago Press, 1934). See also Anselm Strauss's excellent collection, *George Herbert Mead on Social Psychology* (Chicago: University of Chicago Press, 1964). One of the finest sources on the nature of interactionist social psychology is Herbert Blumer's early article, "Social Psychology," in E. P. Schmidt (ed.), *Man and Society* (Englewood Cliffs, N.J.: Prentice-Hall, 1938), pp. 144–98.

2. Charles W. Morris *et al.* (eds.), *The Philosophy of the Act* (Chicago: University of Chicago Press, 1938). Also, A. E. Murphy (ed.), *The Philosophy of the Present* (The Paul Carus Foundation Lectures [Chicago: Open Court, 1932]). Also Merritt H. Moore (ed.), *Movements of Thought in the Nineteenth Century* (Chicago: University of Chicago Press, 1936).

Contents

GEORGE HERBERT MEAD

Essays on His Social Philosophy

George Herbert Mead:
An Introduction

by John W. Petras

AN EXAMINATION of the chronological order of George Herbert Mead's works brings certain consistencies to light. The most notable of these is the shift of interest on his part from social reform, in the early period of his writings, to a later interest in the problems of self-development and the more common psychological research interests such as perception, thought, and the mind. Although the early period is almost entirely devoted to the problems of educational reform, there are implicit ideas that become fully elaborated in the later theory of self-development. First of all, a great deal of attention is focused upon the positive role of play and spontaneity in the total education of the child. As developed later, both of these elements became regarded as indispensable for the normal development of the self. Secondly, the school and the other institutions of society are considered to be part of a larger organic whole, and any separation of them into discrete units is contrary to the nature of the social order. The general progression of Mead's theories, which I shall attempt to make explicit, is from the level of general concepts to the particular example of the general processes he discusses in his philosophy and psychology.

In his first article, Mead chastised the educational system for neglecting the factors of play and spontaneous activity in the classroom. "The purpose of this paper," he wrote, "is to criticize the basing, especially of the earlier education of our children, upon . . . the work phase of activity." [1] As Mead sees it, the problem is one of directing the child's attention to immediate ends in view. This, then, places education in the total universal process of nature, for nature never impels work with reference to an end that has not direct interest. Rather, the task is, at least in part, ". . . accomplished by spontaneous activity

1

. . . by play." [2] Any stimulus presented to the child must be congruent with the level of development of the organism:

> In referring to play, then, as the principle upon which education should be conducted we do not mean that the child should be left to the chance influence of what may be about him, but that we should so arrange their stimuli that they will answer to the natural growth of the child's organism, both as respects the objects he becomes successively interested in and the relations which they have to each other in the life process that he will have to carry out.[3]

What Mead is advocating, therefore, is a solution that falls between the extremes of absolute freedom and determinism, a position that was to become a cornerstone of Dewey's educational philosophy.[4]

In an article that appeared seven years later, Mead demonstrated that his organic view of society had been fairly well formulated by this time.[5] On the basis of the first article, the theme of spontaneity at the general level of society can be recognized. Here Mead criticizes those who would maintain the relationship between the school and society solely upon the basis of the school's financial and political dependence. In order to have a lasting relationship, as well as a meaningful one:

> The vital connection between the school and the home must be social. I do not mean that this relation should not be the ground for most serious thought, but that the home ought to be related to the school, in some real sense a part of it, simply because the children are members of each organization, not because the parents are politically responsible for the existence of the school, not because they have educational theories.[6]

One of the major solutions proposed by Mead to meet both the problem of the relationship between the school and society and the motivation of the child in the classroom was an introduction of the vocational system into the educational network. Chicago at this time found the growing number of second-generation Americans in the school system a particularly pressing problem, and it was mainly because of this situation that Mead stated ". . . we must introduce the vocational motive into our education. . . . We must make the vocation an essential part of the elementary school education." [7] All of these proposals point to what is conceived of as the immediate task of the education:

> . . . to use the child's own impulse, his native interests, material which is worthy because it has meaning for him, and the nature for getting technique which springs from interest in what he does, and

yet to make felt the authoritative discipline and criticism of human achievement, which is as real a part of the child's normal life as it is of the adult; though the incidence is not the same.[8]

What Mead is attempting is to model the educational system after his conception of the higher processes of society. Instruction should become the material of personal intercourse between pupils and instructors as well as between children themselves. It should also substitute ". . . the converse of concrete individuals for the pale abstractions of thought." [9] The relationship to the larger whole is crucial for *the child does not become social by learning. He must be social in order to learn.*[10]

I have presented this brief discussion of Mead's earliest works in order to demonstrate that this theory of the social nature of the individual was first conceived with reference to educational philosophy, not personality development, that is, the theory of the genesis of the self. As mentioned previously, Mead's thought moves from the general conceptual level to the particular, from problems of social reform to problems of individual psychology. Interestingly, this parallels the direction followed in the development of the individual's self, from the social order to the personal order. These early writings, then, provide a framework for understanding Mead's conception of the individual in society. Before continuing, however, I should like to make one further observation concerning the general nature of Mead's writings.

A close examination of his works leaves little doubt that all of them are conceived of in a phylogenetic frame of reference. Mead's persistent usage of the evolutionary perspective in his works is specifically directed to that point in the phylogenetic continuum where man differentiates himself from the rest of the animal kingdom. What I am suggesting is that the theory of self-genesis, the ontogenesis of the self, evolves from the general concept of this perspective. Several major criticisms of Mead have neglected this fact. These criticisms state that Mead failed to deal adequately with the non-rational elements in behavior, and, therefore, was unaware of the important role that such elements played in the development of the self.[11] According to Mead, if we examine the individual within the context of the phylogenetic continuum, one characteristic stands out as a differentiating factor—language. Criticisms of Mead point out that he neglects, by his emphasis on language, the non-vocal forms of communication, and that man uses many such forms—body movements, facial expressions, and gestures, for example. Underlying this criticism is the assumption that the role of language is primarily a communicative role.

3

But Mead did not mean to imply that it was language *as communication* that distinguished man in the phylogenetic continuum. Rather, as Hugh D. Duncan reports ". . . that which distinguishes man from animals is not communication but the ability of men to become objects to themselves through the use of symbols which men themselves *create*, as well as *use*. . . ." [12] Non-vocal communication, therefore, is denied by Mead only where it has no relevance in the processes of self-genesis. Since Mead's theory of self is best understood in relation to aspects of his philosophy of emergence, it will be the final topic of this paper. All other major contributions can be organized under the concepts of mind and society.

Mead sets forth a functional theory of the mind that is similar in all important respects to Dewey's. The mind is defined in terms of function and, as such, exists in a state that finds its reality in behavioral manifestations. The mind exists not as a structure but in a field of conduct that ". . . is not confined to the individual much less located in the brain. Significance belongs to things in their relations to individuals. It does not lie in mental processes which are enclosed within individuals." [13] Mead is at one with the other Pragmatists in his insistence that the mind is a tool, an instrument, that functions to effect a stable relationship between the individual and his environment. [14] The notion that the mind is selective, that it ". . . uses previous experience to determine the nature of the stimulus attended to . . ." [15] follows closely the principles laid down by Dewey in his article on the reflex arc and elaborates upon the conception that consciousness, as it is organized in the individual, may be regarded from the point of view of its objects and the relations of those objects to conduct. [16] Psychology, then, becomes:

> . . . not something that deals with consciousness; psychology deals with the experience of the individual in its relation to conditions under which the experience goes on. It is social psychology where the conditions are social ones. It is behavioristic where the approach to experience is made through conduct. [17]

This relocation of the psychology of the mind into the social order and away from the individual is based upon Mead's introduction of a theory that attempts to account for the growth of the mind. While Mead was greatly influenced by Wilhelm Wundt with regard to the concept of the gesture, he criticized Wundt for his theory of the social order, which presupposed the existence of the mind. Such an explanation, Mead notes, leaves the origin of minds and the interaction among minds mysteries. The mystery is solved:

> If . . . you regard the social process of experience as prior . . .
> to the existence of mind and explain the origin of minds in terms of
> the interaction among individuals among that process, then not only
> the origin of minds, but also the interaction among minds . . .
> cease to seem mysterious or miraculous. Mind arises through communi-
> cation by a conversation of gestures in a social process or context of
> experiences—not communication through mind.[18]

While the mind arises out of the communicative process, its high level
of development in humans depends upon a condition that is separate
from the social order itself, and represents, on the part of Mead, an
ingenious combination of biology, psychology, and sociology. Reflexiveness ". . . is the essential condition, within the social process, for
the development of the mind." [19]

Mead's first discussion of reflexiveness was not directed toward a
particular ability of the human mind, but toward the general societal
process. Thus Mead speaks not of man in the particular, but of all
mankind. Reflective thought, in his early view, was seen as a process
of phylogenetic differentiation that held certain implications for man's
efforts at social reform and control.[20] Although man has a decided
advantage in the evolutionary process once reflective consciousness has
been developed, it does not assure complete control of the social
processes. But it

> . . . puts our own thought and endeavor into the very process of
> evolution, and evolution within consciousness that has become re-
> flective has the advantage over evolution in that the form does not
> tend to perpetuate himself as he is, but identifies himself with the
> process of development. Our reflective consciousness as applied to
> conduct is, therefore, an identification of our effect with the problem
> that presents itself, and the developmental process by which it is
> overcome, and reaches its highest expression in the scientific state-
> ment of the problem, and the recognition and use of scientific method
> and control.[21]

Mead's theory of thought and its processes also followed very
closely those of the other Pragmatists. As with the mind, the outline of
the theory can be seen when taken as a polemic against the theory of
Wundt. Wundt had based his theory upon the aesthetic experience
and believed that ". . . the aesthetic image in the mind or an outer
form, has no function beyond that of responding to and hightening
[sic] the affective experience. . . . If such a statement seems an adequate psychological interpretation of the ideal artist and his creations it
certainly breaks down when applied to primitive art." [22] Thought has
pragmatic and instrumental value. It represents no more than an

internalization of the process that is employed to deal with conflicts and blockages at the social level:

> All analytic thought commences with the presence of problems . . . it continues always to be an expression of such conflict and the solution of the problems involved . . . all reflective thought arises out of real problems present in immediate experience, and is occupied entirely with the solution of these problems or their attempted solution. . . . This solution finally is found in the possibility of the continuing activity, that has been stopped along new or old lines, when such reflective thought ceases in the nature of the case.[23]

As a correlative of thought processes, perception also demands a mediating experience on the part of the subject.[24] As thought itself, perception has instrumental value, and this defines how it is experienced by the individual:

> Every perceived thing is in so far as perceived a recognized means to a possible end, and there can be no hard and fast line drawn between such perceptual consciousness and the more abstracted processes of so-called reasoning. Any form that perceives is in so far carrying on a process of conscious mediation within its act and conscious mediation is ratiocination.[25]

Man's perceptual ability, which is intimately linked with the thought processes, can be traced to differentiations in the evolutionary continuum:

> There are two respects in which the contact experiences of lower animal forms are inferior to those of man for the purpose of perception. The organs of manipulation are not as well adapted in form and function for manipulation itself, and, in the second place, the contact experiences of the lower animals are, to a large extent, determined, not by the process of manipulation, but are so immediately a part of eating, fighting, response, etc., that it is hard to believe that a consciousness of a "thing" can be segregated from these instinctive activities.[26]

The instrumentality of human behavior, which appears at the covert level as thought and perception, is realized at the overt level in the act—the fundamental unit of behavior. This ongoing behavioral process is self-sustaining in the sense that contained within the process is its genesis and consummation. During his lectures, Mead defined the act as ". . . a stimulus and response on the basis of an inner condition which sensitizes the system to the stimulus and quickens the response." [27] The "inner condition" that Mead refers to is a want, or impulse, in the sense of Dewey's usage.[28] Ellsworth Faris refers to these impulses as rooted in the "necessities of life," while others have more explicitly drawn attention to their biological basis.[29] There is, however, no contradiction between these authors and Paul Pfcutzc when the latter notes that ". . . he starts from the outside and works in—emphasizing the act of the individual in its social setting while recognizing those parts of the act which belong to the individual *qua* individual and which do not come to external observation." [30] The act then, is biological in genesis, social in development.

It is at the inter-human plane of interaction where Mead's fullest expression of the emergence of societal behavior from the social act takes place. The initiation of the act commences with the gesture, which is that part of the social act that serves as a stimulus to other forms involved in the same social act.[31] Although the gesture serves to initiate the social act, it does more than merely "trigger" a response on the part of the other forms. In a sense, it lays a blueprint for the consequent emerging behavior. Therefore, its fundamental importance lies in the development of the consciousness of meaning—in reflective thought.[32] The gesture of the first individual in any social act, then, will stimulate the second individual, not through a process of imitation, as James Mark Baldwin had believed, but rather by a process of inter-stimulation in which the participating forms in a social act engage, this leading them functionally together in a common social situation.[33] The gesture, then, always has reference to the future by giving an indication of what is to follow. The act can be seen as teleological in nature only in the sense that its end is present in the beginning as a want. This is of vital importance in understanding the nature of behavior because:

> The teleological or functional nature of the act implies its division into various stages, logically and temporarily related. A purposive activity implies a qualitative change of state as the activity proceeds, e.g. from a hungry to a satiated being. Each state has a value in terms of the function as a whole, according to the extent to which the end is realized in it. A function begins in want or a feeling of incompletion and ends in satisfaction, or a feeling of completion. In between these two feelings is another feeling; that of interest.[34]

It is the response of the second individual that *gives* meaning to the act. That is, the relationship between the stimulus as a gesture and the later phases of the social act constitutes the field within which meaning originates and exists.[35] As shall be seen later, the response of the second individual, his cooperation with the initiator, is necessary for both the development and permanence of the self and society.

As with Cooley and Dewey, among others, Mead presents a view of the individual-society relationship that proceeds on the assumption of mutual dependence.[36] What the environment provided in the sense of meaningful conditions for the direction of the act depends upon the selectivity of the organism. A "thing" becomes recognizable as a *social* object by its potentialities as an element in the selectivity process. In other words, it is defined in terms of function, which means that an object may be defined as a "collapsed act"—the sign of what would happen if the act were carried to completion.[37] On the inter-human level, the completion of the social act indicates the process that makes human society possible. Mead himself writes:

> . . . The very stimulus which one gives to another to carry out his part of the common act affects the individual who so affects the other in the same sense. He tends to arouse the activity in himself which he arouses in the other. He also can in some degree so place himself in the place of the other or the places of others that he can share their experience. Thus the varied means which belong to complicated human society can in varying degrees enter into the experience of many members, and the relationship between the means and the end can enter the experience of the individual.[38]

The phylogenetic distinction that is to be made between the societies of man and the lower forms of animal life is based upon the fact that, at the human level, the operation of society is largely dependent upon a social differentiation that takes the place of the physiological differentiations of the insect. In the latter, the individual end generally fails to expand through communication and participation into the social end that is the *raison d'etre* of the cooperative process.[39] For Mead, then, social conduct becomes that which is mediated by the stimulations of other animals belonging to the same group of living forms, which lead to responses that again affect these other forms.[40] This relationship of co-determinance between the individual and the rest of society has been characterized as one where ". . . the whole is creative of the part, but the part is equally creative of the whole." [41] Society not only exists through inter-stimulation, but inter-stimulation can exist only where there is society. Herbert Blumer has quite forcefully pointed out that Mead's view of society is to be differentiated from the common one that sees man as impinged upon by social forces, that is, where the emphasis is placed upon man as member, not participant. For Mead, on the other hand, the processes of self-indication, as inherent in society, were the major focus.[42] Society represents the macrocosm of all those processes involved in thought, perception, and the interaction of two individuals:

> We must recognize that the most concrete and most fully realized society is not that which is presented in institutions as such, but that which is found is the interplay of social habits and customs, in the readjustment of personal interests that have come into conflict and which take place outside of court, in the changes of social attitude that is not dependent upon an act of legislation.[43]

> Though human attitudes are far older than human institutions and seem to retain identities of structure that make us at home in the heart of every man whose story has come down to us from the written and unwritten past, yet these attitudes take on new forms as they gather new social content.[44]

It is on the assumption that larger social institutions and organizations spring from "multiple social stimulations" in the interaction context, that Mead suggests there is the possibility of smaller group conflicts being absorbed by the larger social order. "There seems to be," he writes:

> . . . an inherent tendency in social groups to advance from the hostile attitudes of individuals and groups toward each other through rivalries, competition, and co-operations toward a functional self-assertion which recognizes and utilizes other selves and groups of selves in the activities in which social human nature expresses itself.[45]

Being rather optimistic, Mead sees the possibility of extending this principle to be the:

> . . . human social ideal—the ideal or ultimate goal of human social progress—the attainment of a universal human society in which all human individuals would possess a perfected social intelligence, such that all social meanings would each be similarly reflected in their respective individual's consciousness—such that the meanings of any one individual's acts or gestures . . . would be the same for any other individual whatever who responded to them.[46]

The gesture most characteristic of human society is the vocal gesture.

As with Dewey, Mead disassociated himself from the early psychological and sociological theories of language. "It arises . . . out of co-operative activities, such as those involved in sex, parenthood, fighting, herding, and the like, in which some phase of the act of one form . . . acts as a stimulus to others to carry on their parts of the social acts." [47] Language is not an affair of the individual, and its laws are generalizations that do not have the slightest meaning if read into terms of the experience of the individual.[48] Language as evolving out of cooperative acts is:

> the first attitude, glance of the eye, movement of the body and its parts indicating the oncoming social act. . . . It becomes language . . . when through his gesture the individual addresses himself as well as the others who are involved in the act. His speech is their speech. He can address himself in their gestures and thus present to himself the whole social situation within which he is involved, so that not only is conduct social but consciousness becomes social as well.[49]

This interaction process through the use of the vocal gesture as the medium of communication is *symbolic interaction*.[50] The role of the symbol in behavior has become more appreciated since Mead first gave it attention, but no one has given a more behavioristic definition than the one he set forth. He writes:

> A symbol is nothing but a stimulus whose response is given in advance. That is all we mean by a symbol. There is a word and a blow. The blow is the historical antecedent of the word, but if the word means an insult, the response is one now involved in the word, something given in the very stimulus itself. That is all that is meant by a symbol.[51]

"What language seems to carry is a set of symbols . . . which is measurably identifiable in the experience of the different individuals." [52] Reason, then, as a cognitive and social process, is the reference to the relations of things by means of symbols. When we are able to indicate these relations by means of these symbols, we get control of them and can isolate the universal characters of things, and the symbols become significant. "No individual . . . which has not come into the use of such symbols is rational. A system of these symbols is . . . language." [53]

The universal nature of language establishes it as the chief mechanism in the development of social control in human society. Concerning this particular aspect of behavior, Mead writes:

> In so far as there are social acts, there are social objects, and I take it that social control is bringing the act of the individual into relation with this social object. . . . Social control, then, will depend upon the degree to which the individual does assume the attitudes of those in the group who are involved with him in his social activities.[54]

As we have seen, the ideal human society would be characterized by complete cognitive agreement among its members as to the meaningful social objects.[55] Essentially, this agreement is to come about through the common recognition of the value of the scientific method as applied to morality. The following quotation is important because it demonstrates Mead's agreement with Dewey on the nature of ethics, and previews his growing interest in a philosophy of emergence and the present:

> We postulate freedom of action as the condition of formulating the ends toward which our conduct shall be directed. Ancient thought assured itself of its ends of conduct and allowed these to determine the world which tested its hypothesis. We insist such ends may not be formulated until we know the field of possible action. The formulation of the ends is essentially a social undertaking and seems to follow the statement of the field of possible conduct, while in fact the statement of the possible field of conduct is actually dependent upon the push toward action. A moving end which is continually reconstructing itself follows upon the continually enlarging field of opportunity of conduct.[56]

Mead, like the other Pragmatists, saw American life as offering the greatest potentiality for the embodiment of this ethic. Here, one found ". . . freedom, within certain rather rigid but very wide boundaries, to work out immediate politics and business with no reverential sense of a pre-existing social order within which they must take their place and whose values they must preserve . . . individualism, perhaps uncouth, but unafraid." [57] The establishment of control and cooperation in such an environment, therefore, depends upon "the degree to which individuals in society are able to assume the attitudes of the others who are involved with them in a common endeavor." [58] How this comes about is the subject of Mead's theory of self-emergence.

I have chosen to treat Mead's theory of self separately from the concepts of mind and society for the following reason. Although it is the best known of his theories as far as sociologists are concerned, it is the most neglected in terms of the context in which it was conceived. This context was provided by Mead's philosophy of the present. My purpose here is to present Mead's theory of self as the crowning example of his philosophy and psychology, as well as the synthesizing element of these two traditions in his thought.

It has been pointed out that Mead's philosophical interests paralleled those of Dewey's most likely because of their mutual interest in social psychology and social reform. The concern with social and educational reform that was so evident in the early works of Mead diminished over time. With Dewey, however, the opposite trend can be observed. Both, however, shared the Pragmatist's concern with the need for an ethics based upon the changing situations of a man's life.[59] While all of the Pragmatists showed a concern for the concept of time, it did not become so large a part of their social theories as it did in the work of Mead. It is Mead's philosophy that allows him to deal with man as determined by his environment and in control of it— both at the same time.

With respect to the concepts of time and change in Pragmatism, William Tremmel writes:

> Here change is not conceived of as necessarily progressive and orderly, but may be complete change, discontinuous and absolutely radical. Change so conceived brings with it the concomitant category of *novelty*. If change is complete, then newness is also complete. In Pragmatism, an event may possess structural characteristics which are absolutely novel. . . . In its basic categories, Pragmatism rejects the ancient principle that nothing can come from nothing. No other world theory asserts change and novelty in so radical a sense.[60]

Time, then, is conceived of in terms of change, and it is defined as the duration of a particular event. Time is a qualitative and not a quantitative feature of the universe. Thus, when I am having a "good" time, the period is different than when I am having a "bad" time, although both may have taken place within the quantitative period which we call "one hour." Schematic time implies that present time is the knife-edged cut of the immediate moment, while experience demonstrates time to be a qualitative spread.[61] Mead's particular theory was set forth in a series of lectures delivered several months before his death. These have been published as *The Philosophy of the Present*:

> The question arises whether the part arising in memory and in the projection of this still further backwards, refers to events which existed as such continuous presents passing into each other, or to that conditioning phase of the passing present which enables us to determine conduct with reference to the future which is also arising in the present. It is this later thesis which I am maintaining.[62]

Mead's theory of time conceived of the past and the future as expansions out of the present, rather than the common conception of a sequence proceeding from the past, to the present, to the future. The reconstruction of the past and the anticipation of the future arise from the same foundation, the reality of the present. The past, therefore, is not a fixed condition of a structured time period, but will vary in accordance with any particular present:

> If we had every possible document and every possible monument from the period of Julius Caesar we should unquestionably have a truer picture of the man and of what occurred in his life-time, but it would be a truth which belongs to this present, and *a later present would reconstruct it from the standpoint of its own emergent nature.*[63]

Immediacy is the keynote of reality, for the past and future that appear in the present may be regarded as merely the thresholds of a minute bit of an unbounded extension whose metaphysical reality reduces the present to an element.[64] Tonness has offered one of the finest summary statements on both the meaning and the relevancy of Mead's theory. Its cogency is best preserved by quoting at length:

> Reality is found in the natural process. The forms of this process, that is, the point at which nature displays its processional character, is the happening events where characters emerge and active existences continue or break. This field of emergent events is the present: the structure of the present is the emergent events, and this structure is basic to time itself. Thus, by this definition, the present becomes the seat of reality. Now, if reality is identified with the process of nature, and if the actuality of this process is in the active and emergent happenings, and if these happenings define the scope of the present, then, of necessity, that which is not in the present because it is not a happening, because it is not in the actuality of the process, must fall outside the field of reality. The former stage of the now on-going process is no longer in activity; it has ceased to exist as process. To say that the former stage is left behind or is past means that its reality ceased when the happenings of that stage expired. The metaphysical reality of the past, therefore, must be denied.[65]

The past, as Murphy points out, may be both novel and irrevocable.[66] Each definite present has its own irrevocable past, but the past is novel for each present. Because of this, Mead is able to state that ". . . the world that comes to us from the past possesses and controls us. We possess and control the world that we discover and invent. . . . This is the world of the moral order." [67] Mead's identification of reality with the process of nature is based upon the fact that an animal is both alive and a part of the physicochemical world. Because of this life is an emergent and extends its influence to the environment about it. *"It is because the conscious individual is both an animal and is*

13

also able to look before and after that consciousness emerges with the meanings and values with which it informs the world." [68]

The notion of the individual's existence in "dual systems" as being important for behavior becomes specifically expressed in the theory of sociality. Lee writes:

> If we define sociality as the presence of a reality in two systems, we see that the individual is social. He belongs to a system which determines him in part, and at the same time to a system which he determines.[69]

Man is part of both the physicochemical world and a social order that precedes him as necessary if he is to develop into a *human* being.

> I wish to emphasize . . . . : The appearance of the self is antedated by the tendencies to take the attitudes of the others, so that the existence of the others is not a reflection of his self-experiences into other individuals. The others are not relative to his self, but his self and the others are relative to the perspective of his self organism.[70]

Since the consciousness of other precedes self consciousness,[71] social consciousness must antedate physical consciousness. "Experience in its original form became reflective in the recognition of selves, and only gradually was there differentiated a reflective experience of things which were purely physical." [72] Finally, the processes of thought and communication became possible only on the presupposition of a social process.[73]

The processes of the self development in the child can be categorized into two general stages that were implicit themes in the early articles on educational philosophy. "The first stage is that of play, and the second that of the game." [74] Play is characterized by spontaneity on the part of the child, by nondeterminacy. Its importance rests with the part it plays in enabling the development of elementary role-taking. Game, on the other hand, results from an internalization of the roles of others. In this sense, it represents a shift from a nondeterminate system to a determinate one.[75] Now at the first of these stages the individual's self is constituted simply by an organization of the particular attitudes of other individuals toward himself and toward one another in the specific social acts in which he participates with them. Game is of the greatest importance because ". . . the animal could never reach the goal of becoming an object to himself as a whole until it could enter into a larger system within which it could play various roles. . . . It is this development that a society whose life process is mediated by communication has made possible. It is here that mental life arises—

with this continual passing from one system to another, with the occupation of both in passage and with the systematic structures that each involves. It is the realm of continual emergence." [76] The self as an object becomes incorporated into the individual:

> . . . through his having assumed the generalized attitude of a member of the group to which that self belongs, a group that widens until it takes in all rational individuals, that is, all individuals who could indicate to one another universal characters and objects in co-operative activity. [77]

The self is comprised of two component processes, the "I" and "Me," which can be seen as representing the dual systems of non-determinacy and determinacy at an internal level. Since life is caught up on an emergent process, the growth of the self arises out of a partial disintegration—the appearance of the different interests in the forum of reflection, the reconstruction of the social world, and the consequent appearances of the new self that answers to the new objects. [78] According to Bittner, the role played by the I in this process is as follows:

> The "I" or the ego is identical with the analytic or synthetic processes of cognition, which in conflicting situations reconstructs out of the "protoplasmic" states of consciousness both the empirical self (the "me") and the world of objects, the objective world is a mental construct and is defined in terms of the needs of the "I" or the ego. [79]

The Me, then, is:

> . . . a man's reply to his own talk. Such a me is not then an early formation which is then projected and ejected into the bodies of other people to give them the breadth of human life. It is rather an importation from the field of social objects into an amorphous, unorganized field of what we call inner experience. Through the organization of this object, the self, this material is itself organized and brought under the control of the individual in the form of so-called self-consciousness. [80]

Thus, the attitude of the social group, the generalized other, provides for the individual a unity of self. In reacting to this attitude, which is established by the community, the individual responds as an I. Behavior, then, proceeds on the basis of this constant process of evaluation, which takes place between the individual and the social group.

What Mead has constructed, therefore, is something more than a theory of behavior and self-development. He has given a theory of self-development that he considers to be congruent with the processes of the universe, the phylogenetic process, and the obvious facts of social life. The primary function of Mead's philosophy was to cast the theory of self into a framework that was bounded by time as well as space. The role of the future, in addition to the past, was recognized as important in the motivation of social behavior. With this, the concept of motivation in the individual and society relationship moved further toward the societal element. For Mead, the role of the individual was one of interpretation of the data furnished him in the social situation. Thus, while the blocked impulse was to be satisfied according to the individual's own desire, his choice of solution was bounded by the fact of his presence in the larger network of society. Social life is to be understood in terms of the principle of co-determination.

Notes to Introduction

1. "The Relation of Play to Education," *University of Chicago Record*, I (1896–1897), 142.

2. *Ibid.*, p. 143.

3. *Ibid.*, p. 145. The application of play and game to the theory of self development first appeared in "The Genesis of the Self and Social Control," *International Journal of Ethics*, XXXV (1924–1925), 251–77.

4. See the author's "John Dewey and the Rise of Interactionism in American Social Theory," *Journal of the History of The Behavioral Sciences*, (in press, 1967).

5. Mead's organic theory of society is at one with the Dewey, Cooley, and Thomas tradition. See Fay Berger Karpf, "Some Social Psychological Contributions of Ellsworth Faris," *Sociology and Social Research*, XXXVIII (1953–1954), 363.

6. Address delivered by Mead as President of the School of Education's Parent's Association, Chicago, December 17, 1903. Published as "The Basis for a Parent's Association," *Elementary School Teacher*, IV (1903–1904), 341.

7. "Exhibit of the City Club Committee on Public Education," *City Club Bulletin*, V (1912), 9. Mead took issue with the traditional curriculum, which had been fashioned after the needs of ". . . the commercial class and for those who expect to pursue literary and professional studies. . . ." ("Industrial Education and the Working Man and the School," *Elementary School Teacher*, IX [1908–1909], 369–83). In 1912, half of the children in Chicago were not completing an elementary education. To Mead, this

represented the lack of meaning and influence of the school itself in the life of children.

8. "Policy of the Elementary School Teacher," *Elementary School Teacher*, VIII (1907–1908), 284. This same year Mead expressed some optimism regarding the reciprocity necessary in any relationship between the school and the larger social order. "It is a sign of good omen for the future that in the place of the school reaching out somewhat helpless hands toward the realities of the life around it, we should find industrial society knocking at the doors of the schoolhouse. . . ." ("Industrial Education and Trade Schools," *Elementary School Teacher* XIII [1907–1908], 406.

9. "Psychology of Social Consciousness Implied in Instruction," *Science*, XXXI (1910), 691. The lack of concreteness in the teaching of science was singled out as especially prevalent. See "Science in the High School," *School Review*, XIV (1906), 243, and "The Teaching of Science in College," *Science*, XXIV (1906), 393.

10. "Psychology of Social Consciousness Implied in Instruction," 693. My emphasis.

11. For example, J. L. Moreno, who states: "For Mead the development of gesture and language occupied too large an area of the psyche leaving little considered and unexplored the *anti*-semantic areas" ("Sociometry and the Social Psychology of George Herbert Mead," *Sociometry*, X [1943], 352).

12. *Communication and Social Order* (New York: The Bedminster Press, 1962), 76.

13. "A Behavioristic Account of the Significant Symbol," *Journal of Philosophy*, XIX (1922), 163.

14. "One of the primary instruments in bringing about redintegration is the notion that the unfinished pushes toward completion, and the incomplete always seeks to be made whole." Ellsworth Faris, "The Social Psychology of George Herbert Mead," *American Journal of Sociology*, XLIII (1937–1938), 402.

15. C. J. Bittner, "George Herbert Mead's Social Concept of the Self," *Sociology and Social Research*, XVI (1931–1932), 7.

16. See John Dewey, "The Reflex Arc Concept in Psychology," *Psychological Review* (1896), 357–70.

17. Charles W. Morris, ed., *Mind, Self, and Society* (Chicago: University of Chicago Press, 1934), 40. Why Mead considered himself to be a "social behaviorist" becomes quite apparent in this statement.

18. *Ibid.*, p. 50.

19. *Ibid.*, p. 134. Note that this ability of man, reflexiveness, lies within the social process that, as will be seen, means the evolutionary or phylogenetic process.

20. Or, as we mentioned earlier, this is the important outgrowth of language that serves as the differentiating element in the phylogenetic continuum, not language as communication. Of further evidence that Mead intended the phylogenetic approach to be employed is his belief that the ultimate cause of reflective consciousness lies in the physiological structure of the human brain as acquired in the evolutionary process. He notes that the central nervous system enables the individual to exercise conscious control over his behavior. "It is the possibility of delayed response which principally differentiates reflective conduct from non-reflective conduct in which the response is always immediate . . ." (*Ibid.*, p. 117).

21. "The Working Hypothesis in Social Reform," *American Journal of Sociology*, V (1899), 371. The implications of reflective consciousness for social control were expanded in a later book review by Mead. "The point that needs to be emphasized is that reflective consciousness, when it meets an essential difficulty and forms an hypothesis to solve this problem, has just the same attitude toward its social theories as that which it holds toward physical theories. . . . The whole body of knowledge is open to reconstruction" (Review of D. Draghicesco, *Du Rôle de L'individu dans le déterminisme social*, and *Le probleme du déterminisme, déterminisme biologique et déterminisme social*, appearing in *Psychological Bulletin*, II [1905], 405).

22. "The Imagination in Wundt's Treatment of Myth and Religion," *Psychological Bulletin*, III (1906), 399.

23. "Suggestions Toward a Theory of the Philosophical Disciplines," *Philosophical Review*, IX (1900), 2. Mead also writes, "Thinking is simply the reasoning of the individual, the carrying on of a conversation between what I have termed the 'I' and the 'me'" (*Mind, Self, and Society*, 335).

24. See abstract, "The Relation of Imitation to the Theory of Animal Perception," *Psychological Bulletin*, IV (1907), 210–11.

25. "Concerning Animal Perception," *Psychological Review*, XIV (1907), 390. Morris points out that, for Mead, response to a perceived object has three phases, the actual perception being only the first. The following phases are manipulatory and consummatory. Introduction to *The Philosophy of the Act* (Chicago: University of Chicago Press, 1938), xxv–xxvi.

26. *Ibid.*, p. 388.

27. From notes of Herbert Blumer, taken in lectures on social psychology given by George Herbert Mead (courtesy of Joseph Zygmunt). The key phrase here, as opposed to Watsonian behaviorism, is "sensitizes the system to the stimulus." Once it is sensitized, thought and perception enter. For

Watson's own statement of the classical behaviorist position, see "Psychology and Behaviorism," *Psychological Review*, XX (1913), 158–77.

28. That is, it is not to be confused with instinct. The difference is that the impulse does not impel toward a specific goal as is implied in instinct. For the act to be carried to completion, the impulse must be structured by the social situation as mediated by the actor.

29. Faris, *op. cit.*, in Note 14, above, 393. Faris speaks of "the activities of those who hunger," and so forth. For those who speak more freely of a biological base, see Nelson Foote and Leonard S. Cottrell, *Identity and Interpersonal Competence* (Chicago: University of Chicago Press, 1955), 58, and Heinz Mauss, *A Short History of Sociology* (London: Routledge and Kegan Paul, 1962), 106.

30. *Self, Society, Existence* (New York: Harper and Brothers, 1961), 45.

31. *Mind, Self, and Society*, 42. Again, confusion can arise if the phylogenetic and ontogenetic perspectives of Mead are not analytically separated. In the particular system, the ontogenetic, the gesture is the initiator of the social act. In the general system, the phylogenetic, it is seen as a preliminary step in the development of language and here the gesture is an affective expression. "However necessary it is for a language of gesture that it should raise itself above this stage, it remains true that it would never have arisen without the original emotional impulse" ("The Relations of Psychology and Philology," *Psychological Bulletin*, I [1904], 380).

32. "What Social Objects Must Psychology Presuppose?" *Journal of Philosophy*, VII (1910), 178. This is what Mead means when he says, "The later stages of the act are all ready to go off, but in the sense that they serve to control the process itself" (*Mind, Self, and Society*, 11).

33. Fay Berger Karpf, *American Social Psychology* (New York: McGraw-Hill Book Co., 1932), 320.

34. Grace Chin Lee, *George Herbert Mead, Philosopher of the Social Individual* (New York: King's Crown Press, 1945), 14.

35. W. L. Troyer, "Mead's Social and Functional Theory of Mind," *American Sociological Review*, XI (1946), 201. Troyer goes on to note, "What is particularly of significance in such a statement is that meaning, as thus considered, is a development *objectively there* as a relation between certain phases of the social act. It is not to be thought of as a 'psychical addition' to the act. . . ."

36. Swanson writes, "Mead's account opposes the view that conduct is determined solely by the organism or by the environment. It is not opposed in principle to a deterministic view of behavior. Organic necessities and past experience determine the hypotheses which the organism advances in the early stages of action. Once stimuli are constituted, they write their responses to the organism's proposals in a firm, round, determining hand"

("Mead and Freud: Their Relevance for Social Psychology," *Sociometry*, XXIV [1961], 327).

I think Swanson's argument could be modified if the act is seen in the context of Mead's philosophy of the present, which will be discussed later. Although the impulses do determine the hypotheses, this entire process lies in the realm of the universal processes of emergence. The act is incomplete because it is part of this process where part of its action is always in the future. In this sense, all is determined.

37. W. L. Troyer, *op. cit.*, p. 202. Objects, in other words, have no meaning apart from their function.

38. *The Philosophy of the Act*, 137.

39. *Ibid.*

40. "The Mechanism of Social Consciousness," *Journal of Philosophy*, IX (1912), 401.

41. William C. Tremmel, "The Social Concepts of George Herbert Mead," *The Emphoria State Research Studies*, IV (1957), 10. This article is one of the few available that treats Mead primarily as a philosopher who was interested in social conduct.

42. Herbert Blumer, "Society as Symbolic Interaction," in Arnold Rose (ed.), *Human Behavior and Social Processes* (Boston: Houghton Mifflin Co., 1962), 179–92.

43. "Natural Right and the Theory of Political Institutions," *Journal of Philosophy*, XII (1915), 152.

44. "The Psychology of Punitive Justice," *American Journal of Sociology*, XXIII (1917–1918), 592–93.

45. *Ibid.*, pp. 593–94.

46. *Mind, Self, and Society*, 310. In the spirit of William James, Mead attacks the Spencerians for their implicit fatalism regarding the phylogenetic process. The emphasis upon mere adjustment was contrary to one of the cardinal principles of Pragmatism—the notion that man could control his environment. "Spencer misinterpreted evolution as a process of bare adaptation. His picture of the goal of social evolution as a society in which men are completely adapted to their physical and social environment would certainly inspire no enthusiasm of endeavor, even if it could be got into men's minds. And if, as Bergson insists, even biological evolution is creative, then beyond doubt this is the case in social evolution" (*The Philosophy of the Act*, 506).

47. *The Philosophy of the Present* (Chicago: Open Court, 1932), 167. It should be noted that Dewey's theory of language is essentially the same as Mead's, and several aspects of it precede some of Mead's work. I think

that the reason Mead, rather than Dewey, is best remembered in this connection is the theory of self. Language is an indispensable aspect of this theory, and it is for this theory which Mead is best known in sociological circles. On the other hand, as far as sociologists have been concerned, Dewey left no such characteristic contribution.

48. "The Relations of Psychology and Philology," 377.

49. "The Psychology of Punitive Justice," 578–79.

50. It must be remembered, however, that the crucial role played by language at the human level rests not in its function as a communicative device with others, but as an *intra*-individual communicative instrument.

51. *Mind, Self, and Society*, 181. Or, "When . . . gesture means this idea behind it and it arouses that idea in the other individual, then we have a significant symbol" (*ibid.*, p. 45).

52. *Ibid.*, p. 54.

53. *The Philosophy of the Act*, 518. Given the intimate relationship between symbols and the reasoning process as mediated by language, various studies have demonstrated that a disruption of the vocal aspect of behavior will lead to disruptions in the cognitive processes. For the classic study in this regard, see H. Head, *Aphasia and Kindred Disorders of Speech* (2 vols.; New York: Macmillan, 1926).

54. "The Genesis of the Self and Social Control" (see Note 3), 273 and 274. The notion that social control was something that the individual internalized, if it is to be effective, was the great advance of Ross over Durkheim, according to Mauss. It might be added, then, that Mead's advance over Ross was one of indicating the processes involved. See Mauss, *op. cit.*, p. 102.

55. Here language is indispensable. As Morris notes, "Objects which are capable of controlling overt responses if an organism were at the objects, even though the organism can never directly confront them, are still regarded as perceptual objects" (Introduction to *The Philosophy of the Act*, xviii).

56. "Scientific Method and the Individual Thinker," in John Dewey, *et al.* (eds.), *Creative Intelligence* (New York: Henry Holt, 1917), 224.

57. "The Philosophies of Royce, James, and Dewey in Their American Setting," in William H. Kilpatrick and Henry R. Linwell (eds.), *John Dewey: The Man and His Philosophy* (Cambridge: Harvard University Press, 1930), 104.

58. "The Genesis of the Self and Social Control," *op. cit.*, p. 275.

59. Mead's fullest exposition of his own theory of ethics is contained in "The Philosophical Basis of Ethics," *International Journal of Ethics*, XVIII (1908), 311–23. He adds an interesting dimension to the criticism

of an ethics based upon an external moral ideal: "Not only does an external moral ideal rob immediate moral conduct of its most important values, but it robs human nature of the most profound solace which can come to those who suffer—the knowledge that the loss and the suffering, with its subjective poignancy, has served to evaluate conduct, to determine what is and what is not worthwhile" (ibid., p. 323).

60. Tremmel, op. cit., p. 7.

61. Ibid., p. 9. As Martindale notes, William James had a great deal of influence upon Mead in this regard. In James, the theory of time was first presented in The Principles of Psychology in his discussion of "streams of consciousness." See D. Martindale, The Nature and Types of Sociological Theory (Boston: Houghton Mifflin, 1960), 341. Mead was also heavily influenced by Royce with regard to the concepts of time and self, and acknowledged his debt to him in "Josiah Royce—A Personal Impression," International Journal of Ethics, XXVII (1917), 168–70. An appreciation of the richness of Royce's theories can be obtained from the excellent secondary source by James H. Cotton, Royce on the Human Self (Cambridge: Harvard University Press, 1954).

62. The Philosophy of the Present, 28–29. "The past is a past of the present and the future is a future of the present" (David Miller, "G. H. Mead's Conception of the Present," Philosophy of Science, X [1943], 42). "Any given past is the past of a definite present" (Alfred Tonness, "A Notation on the Problem of the Past—With Empirical Reference to George Herbert Mead," Journal of Philosophy, XXIX [1932], 606).

63. The Philosophy of the Present, 31. My emphasis.

64. Ibid., p. 32.

65. Tonness, "A Notation on the Problem of the Past . . . ," loc. cit., p. 601.

66. Arthur E. Murphy, Introduction to The Philosophy of the Present, xviii.

67. "Scientific Method and the Moral Sciences," International Journal of Ethics, XXXIII (1932), 247.

68. The Philosophy of the Present, 66. My emphasis.

69. Op. cit., p. 9. Sociality, for Mead, was more than a social psychological principle. "Mead's extension of this principle to the universe as a whole was perhaps his most original and daring postulation. He came to believe that there is 'sociality' in nature; and thus he made the claim that the highest and finest product of the whole evolutionary process is the ideal of human solidarity, cooperation, justice and mutual service. The appearance of 'minds' and 'selves' is only the culmination of that sociality which is found throughout the universe" (Paul E. Pfeutze, op. cit., p. 64).

70. *The Philosophy of the Act,* 153.

71. Bittner, *op. cit.,* p. 17.

72. "What Social Objects Must Psychology Presuppose?", 180.

73. *Mind, Self, and Society,* 260.

74. "The Genesis of the Self and Social Control," 269.

75. It should be noted that the concept of taking the other's role as important in the development of the self was all but made explicit in the works of Baldwin. It seems that many third parties who are eager to demonstrate the advances of Mead over Baldwin give the latter much less credit for his influences than Mead did himself. Mead wrote that Baldwin ". . . had described as satisfactorily as any psychologist, the process by which the child's own personality arises out of the differentiation of a general social consciousness into an ego and alii. In "Review of D. Draghicesco . . . ," *op. cit.,* pp. 403–404. Whereas Mead saw the histrionic tendency as natural to man, Baldwin saw imitation as a natural tendency.

76. *The Philosophy of the Present,* 85.

77. *The Philosophy of the Act,* 375. "The multiple social stimulations of an indefinite number of varied contacts of a vast number of individuals with each other is the fertile field out of which spring social organizations, for these make possible the larger social life that can absorb the hostilities of different groups" ("The Psychology of Punitive Justice," 593). Lee writes, "Because all individuals participate in functional groups . . . the basis exists for their development of a social attitude. A social attitude is one involving the recognition by the individual that he is not alone in the world but exists among other individuals" (*op. cit.,* pp. 36–37). In view of this, it is easy to understand why Mead considered the problem of war to be a psychological problem whose solution depended upon further extension of these cooperative tendencies. See "The Psychological Bases of Internationalism," Survey XXXIII (1914–1915), 604–607. The extension of this principle on a more local level was used as partially explaining philanthropy. See "Philanthropy From the Point of View of Ethics," in E. Faris, *et al.* (ed.), *Intelligent Philanthropy* (Chicago: University of Chicago Press, 1930), 133–48.

78. "The Social Self," 379.

79. *Op. cit.,* p. 11.

80. "The Mechanism of Social Consciousness," 405.

1

The Policy of the Elementary
School Teacher*

T HE LOSS TO THIS JOURNAL of Professor Wilbur S. Jackman has
brought with it the problem of responsibility for the further
conduct of the *Elementary School Teacher* and its policy. Professor
Jackman's editorials represented very vividly not only his own reactions
to the problems of elementary education, but also that liberating movement in pedagogy for which Mr. Jackman and Colonel Parker before
him have stood. The numbers which have appeared since Mr. Jackman's
death have sought to continue the spirit and form with which he had
invested the publication. It was however characteristic of its former
editor's direction that the *Elementary School Teacher* reflected not
only an educational movement but also an embodiment of this movement in a personality.

Such a direction cannot be long successfully continued when the
personality has gone. While, therefore, the journal continues to represent the liberalizing movement in education with which Mr. Jackman
identified himself, the responsibility for its presentation has been
divided among those who we hope will be competent to represent its
many sides. The editing of the *Elementary School Teacher* has passed,
then, into the hands of a committee, made up from the department of
Philosophy and Education in the University of Chicago, and from the
staffs of the University's College of Education and the Elementary
School. We have sought safety in numbers, recognizing the bewilderingly

* As originally published in the *Elementary School Teacher*, VIII (1907–
1908), 281–84.

numerous phases of elementary-school teaching and the importance of the specialist in representing these to the public whom we seek to reach. The editorial committe is a part of a larger one including that which conducts the *School Review.* The conduct of the *Elementary School Teacher* will therefore have the benefit of association with an organ representing secondary education. There should result from this association broader views of problems which are common to both the elementary and high schools, and an increased confidence in presenting to those interested in elementary teaching the course which modern pedagogy should steer among its perplexing problems.

There is little difficulty in formulating the programme of the modern pedagogy. It calls for a school so organized socially that the child may live there his own life. The experiences of school life are to be justified by their immediate value to the children as well as by their import for the activities of adults. This sort of education takes place at home—it is the only education among more primitive peoples. Its results justify the method. The character-building, the unfolding of balanced intelligence which a well-ordered home achieves, present an educational ideal which perhaps no elementary schools have ever reached. What is more natural than to demand that family life be domesticated in the schoolhouse? But in the average schoolhouse we find a régime organized with an eye single to the acquirements demanded by the after life of the man and the woman. The pupil is looked at under the perspective of the adult. It is easy to react against this unnatural attitude, by substituting for the adult interests, which are overrepresented in typical curriculums, the interests of the child; to find in the spontaneous activities of childhood the subject-matter for the child's curriculum.

This reaction, however, overlooks the morale of family life. It is the dominant activity of the parents that constitutes the control, that determines times and seasons, and gives the proper perspective to the child's interest. When the child helps in the labors of the home, or bears his part in the industries that used to center there, an educational ideal arises, which could only be realized in the school if its activities had the same compelling power. To make the school life entirely out of the child's spontaneous processes is to quite upset the natural order of the family or community life which we are seeking to copy. Education in these its natural habitats consists in relating the child's spontaneous activities to the dominant, controlling activities of the community. It is the presence of this relation in trade and professional schools that gives a morale to their pupils which is indeed purchased at the price of a certain unfortunate narrowness.

The doors by which educational reform entered the school were those of history, the sciences, and nature-study. Today we see both a development of this reform and a reaction against it. The industrial arts have come to take the strategic position which history and nature-study earlier occupied. The reason for this is evident. The arts give a powerful motive to the child for acquiring technique, by means of which it is hoped that the desired control over language and number may be gained. The reaction is represented by the demand for drill as the pivotal element of the school teaching. It appears in the guise of modern psychology, in the demand for habits which will operate without conscious attention, or for the education of the spinal column with its reflexes and automatisms. On the one hand this reaction demands the old methods of instruction in language and number, and has no confidence in the motives that spring from the child's desire to gain skill, and to acquire techniques. On the other hand the movement has behind it the feeling that a school which follows simply the creative and outgoing impulses of the children lacks the compulsion which the child's activities at home, on the farm, and in the shop, meet in adjusting themselves to the adult processes to which they contribute.

The school which merely drills is hopelessly isolated from the real life of the child. And we must make the same criticism upon a school life which is organized entirely about outgoing and creative impulses. A child who criticizes the results of his work with the severity of the artist and skilled mechanic is no longer a child. The child, because he is a child, is more interested in the process than in the result.

Here lies the crux of the problem in elementary education: How to use the child's own impulses, his native interests, material which is worthy because it has meaning for him, and the motive for getting technique which springs from interest in what he does, and yet to make felt the authoritative discipline and criticism of adult human achievement, which is as real a part of the child's normal life as it is of the adult's, though the incidence is not the same.

While this journal has no fixed programme to proclaim, it will continue to stand for modern educational reform in both the phases above stated, regarding with especial interest the movement toward social organization of the school as a means to the attainment of the disciplinary element in the child's development.

2

The Relation of Play to Education*

THERE ARE THREE GENERAL TYPES of human activity, work, art, and play. We may define work as an endeavor, in which a definite end is set up, and the means are chosen solely with reference to that end. In art the control of the activity is not a sharply defined end which governs the selection of the means, but the harmony of the means in their relation to each other. A true work of art arouses pleasure because of the perfection of the construction and consequent truth of the representation. But it would be a false psychological analysis to assume that this end is in the consciousness of the artist, consequently guiding his selection of the means at his disposal. In the successful activity of the artist the thought of the public as pleased or bored by his production would be only so much hindrance. He has nothing to depend upon but the feeling of appropriateness and consistency in the means which he uses for the expression of his idea. The expression of the idea is the impulse to his activity but it is not an end in the sense of a consciously defined ideal object which in itself determines all the means used. The expression of the artist's idea can be clearly defined in his own mind only when the product is practically accomplished. In art then we may say that the attention is fixed upon means and their relations, in other words upon the *technique*. Play finally distinguishes itself from both work and art in its absolute spontaneity and in its lack of consciousness of an end in view, of the means used to accomplish an end, or finally of the perfection of the movements and postures, that is of the technique. Of course an end is accomplished by play, but the health and grace of movement, the social ease and general

* As originally published in the *University of Chicago Record*, I (1896–1897), 140–45.

development that follow from play under favorable circumstances can never occupy the attention of the children, nor yet can they select their plays nor the instruments which they use in them with a view to such ends. The whole spontaneity and with it the fascination and value of play would be lost if such elements were brought to the child's consciousness.

This is not saying that these typical activities do not overlap each other. There are points in all endeavor when either work or art becomes play for the time being. It is an unfortunate workman who is in no sense an artist, and a sorry artist who never works. Finally it is possible to conceive abstractly of conditions in which all endeavor should have the spontaneity of play, should be accompanied by the artist's consciousness of the harmonious interrelation of all the activities that go to bring about the result, and yet all have the rational consequence of a piece of well considered and adequately planned work. But this overlapping and conceivable coincidence of these different phases does not blur the distinctions between them as we watch them in the lives of others and ourselves.

Now our education, at least beyond the primary grade and before it reaches the laboratory or the experimental method, depends solely upon the work phase of human activity for the development of the child. I refer to consciously directed education and to the general drift of our methods and schools. There are notable exceptions to be found here and there, but they remain exceptions. There is as indicated a great deal of wholesome common sense which recognizes, without formulating it, the tremendous value that accrues to children from play and is willing ungrudgingly to sacrifice often the supposed advantages of regulated work in the school room for the freedom of development and generosity of interest which comes with an out of door life under favorable circumstances. I know personally a professor in Columbia University whose mother kept him out of school till he was twelve years old and left him with his interests in insects and flowers, in tools and playthings, and withal not very much directed. Similar instances are familiar, I presume, to many of us, but they are still but exceptions to the general principles that guide our education. It is the purpose of this paper to criticize the basing, especially of the earlier education of our children, upon this work phase of our activity.

Two classes of labor from time immemorial have been recognized, the free and the slave labor. Slave labor is no longer recognized in the statute-books of any civilized nation, but in the most highly civilized lands the labor-agitators are never weary of asserting that in character labor remains essentially slavish. What is the fundamental distinction between free and slave labor?

We certainly do not mean by free labor that the workman is to be left free to follow any whim which chances to root itself in his mind. The labor is to be directed as really under a system of free labor as under one of slave labor. The distinction does not lie in the presence or absence of determining direction, but in the nature of the means by which that direction is enforced. The motive of wages, with the consequent support of the laborer and his family and the possibility of rising by accumulations and increased skill, are the means used, instead of the whip. It is, however, evident that the motive power is still outside the activity of the laborer. Hunger or even hope of advancement in life represents still a *vis a tergo,* so far as the particular piece of work is concerned. So long as intelligent interest in the product to be attained is not the immediate motive power in holding the laborer to his work, it is slave labor, according to the definition that Aristotle gave of it. The only distinction lies in the fact that Aristotle supposed that those, whose intelligent interest could not be aroused in the work, must be politically subject to those who directed them.

Although this may not be recognized in so many words, the great advantage which branches of labor have, that involve high mechanical or some artistic power, lies in this interest of the laborer in the work itself. Labor troubles are comparatively absent from these callings, and the relation of employers and employed is much more satisfactory and intimate than in the callings in which the employer can depend only upon the bread and butter earning character of the wage to hold the workman to his task. Profit-sharing means a similar invasion of this field of essentially slave labor, and where it can be successfully undertaken the added zest of the workmen speak eloquently for the opening up of new and more natural motive power.

It is then impossible to get beyond this incomplete and unnatural character of work until the whole man responds immediately to the product upon which he is working, and is not required to seek for impetus in his labor from an interest that lies completely outside his shop or factory and its activities. This does not mean, of course, that the workman is to lose all thought of those that are dependent upon him, and all that flows to him and them from his ultimate success, but that there should be no break between the two sources of interest, any more than there should be in the life of the successful business and professional man, though here the chasm is by no means completely bridged. In other words, in an ideal condition the interest which directs any separate activity should be but an expression of the whole interest in life and carry the momentum with it of this whole. Until this is attained labor cannot become entirely free.

We are not, of course, interested at present in the probability or the improbability of the coming of such a millennium. The advantage for us of the recognition of the different sorts of labor lies in the possibility of discussing the legitimacy of the application of the principle of work to education. We are not able to reconstruct our whole industrial system so that the labor shall be always an expression of the whole man, but we are able to banish this slavish, dwarfing method from our school rooms.

The unfortunate character of the method comes out most clearly when we consider it from the standpoint of the physiology of the nervous system. As we know now, the cells in the brain at birth are practically all complete, but the connections between the cells—the so-called coördinations—have yet to be established, at least in large measure. Indeed this process goes on at least till the age of twenty-five, and perhaps much later. It is the formation of these coördinations that represents on the side of the nervous systems the process of education. The question at once suggests itself, how can they be set up? Is the brain an empty country into which the educator can go, like the manager of a telegraph company, and put wires where he will? Is it possible for him to break through paths in the brain at any point that suits his fancy, or, if you like, his pedagogical sense? Is it possible to force a path through by pure force of drilling along lines to which the child shows no capacity? Or is it a question of what the Germans call *Anlage*, or a natural capacity? Or, to put the question in still a different form, is there an essential difference in the development of the body after and before birth? The surrounding mother form affords before birth the appropriate conditions and stimuli for the development of the embryo. Does society do more than to receive the child into favorable conditions and afford the appropriate stimuli for the development of the still imperfect child form? So far as we know the mother form provides simply favorable conditions for development, plus the stimulus of a highly organized food medium. Can society legitimately attempt to do more than the mother form in principle? And yet when society employs the method of work as the method of education it is taking a completely different course from that which is pursued by nature before birth.

To comprehend this we must remember that the brain coördinations are organs of the body as really as the lungs or the heart, that they have their essential value in the development of the whole organism as really as the liver or the intestines. Now so far as we understand the development of the embryo the stimulus is at first food, and not until the organ is comparatively highly developed does the stimulus of use come in. This comes out very clearly in the evolution of such functions as those of walking after birth. There is a steady development of the coördinations in the brain which call forth this activity, but the process itself is not called into action until the coördination is practically formed. Take a child seven or eight months old and hold its feet on a smooth table and he will move them rhythmically, showing that the coördination has already largely broken through. But nature does not at once place the necessity of walking upon the child in order to insure the skill of the older child in walking. She lets him kick his legs as much as he will. That is, she allows him to play, and out of this play arises all of the exercise that is needed. What needs to be noticed here is that this play does not direct the child's attention to any end to be accomplished by the use of the limbs. In other words the stimulus of use does not arise under normal circumstances until the organ is so far developed that its use becomes a natural and essential part of the activity of the whole body. Nowhere in the development before birth and immediately afterwards, nor anywhere, where our instruction does not come in, is an organ *used* simply with a view to a function that is to come later. Or, to put it in terms that we used earlier, nature never compels work with reference to an end which has not direct interest, while the young form is developing. She accomplishes her part of the task by spontaneous activity, in other words by play, while we feel it necessary to arouse the stimulus of use before the organ is capable of being used in the only sense in which an organ should be used. When an organ is properly used, when it is fully and normally developed, any exercise of it should be one of the entire organism through it, that is the whole interest that is involved in the entire life process should come to expression in that one function. Play is the application of this principle to development.

Undoubtedly in play, an exercise is given to as yet imperfectly developed organs, but it never involves a directing end or purpose which lies in its full expression beyond the capacity of the organism in its present state of development. For example a kitten playing with a spool undoubtedly represents an exercise of the functions of mouse catching, which is of great value to the full developed animal; but the point is that nature neither makes the kitten dependent upon the use of its yet imperfect capacity in order to stimulate it to higher development, nor yet does she in any way test the success of any separate part of the act by the criterion of adult mouse catching. The playing with the spool stands upon the same plane of development as the kitten, and there is no control exercised over it by the completed act of mouse catching, except in the sense that the spool calls out spontaneously all the mouse-catching capacity of the kitten at her present stage of advancement.

As fast as these coördinations begin to ripen there is abundance of

31

nerve force to keep them exercised. It is the most evident characteristic of childhood that there is a superabundance of energy, required for no immediate purpose, that brings to expression each new capacity of the infant-form as soon as it is consistent with the entire life-process of the organism. In other words under normal conditions the child's life should be perfectly homogeneous; either it is made up of the pursuit of ends which are perfectly comprehensible to the child and of native interest to him, or else of spontaneous outbursts of activities that represent newly formed coördinations, whose meaning is not yet fully evident and will not perhaps become so till the form has become adult. So far as the immediate life of the child is concerned and its consciousness, they have no value except as escape valves for the surplus energy. They are purely spontaneous. From the standpoint of the final development of the child they mean the taking possession of and making itself at home in new-won coördinations, that are later to be of the highest value to the man.

It is evident that nature, then, never uses the principle of work as that upon which to forward development. I am referring of course to as yet undifferentiated functions. What the child comprehends and can do, it will do with a native interest that requires no continuous spurring. But this occupies but a small part of the child's life. Nature depends upon the presence simply of the right stimuli to call out spontaneous use of new coördinations as fast as formed. And this is, in principle, play. As a part of the supporting and developing social form for the yet dependent child, it is our duty to see that the requisite nourishment and protection for the continued growth of the child is present, and then that those stimuli are not lacking which answer to the developing coördinations of the central nervous system, and which will call out spontaneously the exercise of these functions. In a word the whole education of a child should be upon the principle of teaching him to walk. We do not put him through a carefully controlled series of leg motions from birth on that he may have the necessary facility later. We simply see that there are an abundance of chairs and other objects by which he can pull himself up, a floor adapted to stimulating the soles of the feet and things that he wants at a distance. There is nothing else to be done in teaching the use of number or any other branch so far as the principle is concerned.

The matter is simple enough so far as the walking is concerned, for these means are right at hand. The problem becomes much more complicated when we reach higher stages of development. A moving object is all that is necessary for the education of a kitten. But the life of the man is infinitely complicated in comparison with that of the cat, and the series of stimuli that are needed for his education are proportionately more numerous and complex. I think that it is fair to say that in an ideally constructed society these stimuli would be as naturally present, as are those which bring about the education in walking. But it is just the characteristics of our society that it is not perfect and that it is the child *par excellence*, that forces upon us the recognition of this lack of perfection, and makes us, with reference to him, try to provide a minature society which shall be as near perfection as possible. The environment of the child, as providing the appropriate stimuli to call out the exercise of all the functions of the child in succession as they appear, would represent, in miniature, at least the normal environments, physical and social, of the man. The problem of educating the child is almost as large as that of accomplishing the full development of society, representing an earlier stage in the accomplishment of the latter. It is still true that "a little child shall lead them."

As far as system is concerned it is a great deal easier to simply drill a child a year on all the combinations of numbers up to five, than it is to find out how and when he naturally begins to recognize the numerical distinctions, and to provide the natural stimuli to which these coördinations will respond. Miss Allyn did it, for example, in Mrs. Quincy-Shaw's school, some years ago, by the use of coins. Upon them as stimuli the child responded gradually with a whole series of combinations. It was not for the purpose of actually buying and selling. It was simply playing at buying and selling. It was a purely spontaneous activity, but one that was essential for the child, if he was to take possession, so to speak, of these new brain coördinations, just as a smooth floor and objects by which to pull himself up are essential to the child if he is to walk. No one can tell him how to use his limbs, but one can put chairs in his way and hold out to him an apple at a little distance. If he have no stimuli he will never walk, but the stimuli do nothing more than enable him to do what he is all ready to do.

The problem is to find the appropriate stimulus which naturally calls out the activity as far as it is then developed, not to get hold of motives which will force the child to work where he has and can have no interest. The final solution of the problem is surrounding the child with the life process in such a form that it will appeal to him. In Sloyd work or the simple use of carpenter's tools, in molding objects from the history of the race, in the presentation of industrial processes, in the watching and care for insects and animals, there lies an abundance of stimuli for all the developing child's powers, not presented in a helter-skelter fashion but arranged and united in such a way that the child responds to their values for life, as he gradually awakes to them. For, to continue our terminology, a child is forming, in the central

33

nervous system, not only simple coördinations but coördinations of coördinations, and there must be the stimuli for these latter as much as for the former. The problem is by no means a simple one, but this is no excuse for continuing the old method of giving him his whole technique of life in advance, before he can have any objects on which to use them.

For this is our method at present. We aim to give a child *methods* while his interest is all in objects. He wants the natural stimuli, and we insist on forcing through coördinations of our own making. This method is of course subject to a fundamental psychological fallacy. We try to fix the child's attention upon the problem we set him, and really we are fixing it upon the external motives which are to keep him at work. The result is that he loses, frequently, the power of real concentration. How many of us can add a long column without making a number of errors? We are unable practically to keep the attention upon so simple a process continually, while in something that has our whole interest from the start, which we have learned under the influence of this interest, there may be no break in the process from beginning to end. I am sure that this very common disability comes from the constant break that must take place in the child's study of arithmetic as it is usually taught. He must be continually jumping back from the study that has no interest for him to the discipline of the school that keeps him at work. We are setting up coördinations here but, instead of their being between the different steps of the problem, they lie from one step to the teacher's eye or the fear of staying after school and back again. Those we set up are making constant breaks in the coördinations we wish to form.

In referring to play, then, as the principle upon which education should be conducted we do not mean that the child should be left to the chance influence of what may be about him, but that we should so arrange these stimuli that they will answer to the natural growth of the child's organism, both as respects the objects he becomes successively interested in and the relations which they have to each other in the life process that he will have to carry out.

3

The Psychology of Social Consciousness Implied in Instruction*

I HAVE BEEN ASKED to present the social situation in the school as the subject of a possible scientific study and control.

The same situation among primitive people is scientifically studied by the sociologist (folk-psychologist). He notes two methods in the process of primitive education. The first is generally described as that of play and imitation. The impulses of the children find their expression in play, and play describes the attitude of the child's consciousness. Imitation defines the form of unconscious social control exercised by the community over the expression of childish impulse.

In the long ceremonies of initiation education assumed a more conscious and almost deliberate form. The boy was induced into the clan mysteries, into the mythology and social procedure of the community, under an emotional tension which was skilfully aroused and maintained. He was subjected to tests of endurance which were calculated not only to fulfil this purpose, but also to identify the ends and interests of the individual with those of the social group. These more general purposes of the initiatory ceremonies were also at times cunningly adapted to enhance the authority of the medicine man or the control over food and women by the older men in the community.

Whatever opinion one may hold of the interpretation which folk-psychology and anthropology have given of this early phase of education, no one would deny, I imagine, the possibility of studying the education of the savage child scientifically, nor that this would be a psychological

* As originally published in *Science*, XXXI (1910), 688–93.

study. Imitation, play, emotional tensions favoring the acquirement of clan myths and cults, and the formation of clan judgments of evaluation, these must be all interpreted and formulated by some form of psychology. The particular form which has dealt with these phenomena and processes is social psychology. The important features of the situation would be found not in the structure of the idea to be assimilated considered as material of instruction for any child, nor in the lines of association which would guarantee their abiding in consciousness. They would be found in the impulse of the children expressed in play, in the tendency of the children to put themselves in the place of the men and women of the group, i.e., to imitate them in the emotions which consciousness of themselves in their relationship to others evoke, and in the import for the boy which the ideas and cults would have when surcharged with such emotions.

If we turn to our system of education we find that the materials of the curriculum have been presented as percepts capable of being assimilated by the nature of their content to other contents in consciousness, and the manner has been indicated in which this material can be most favorably prepared for such assimilation. This type of psychological treatment of material and the lesson is recognized at once as Herbartian. It is an associational type of psychology. Its critics add that it is intellectualistic. In any case it is not a social psychology, for the child is not primarily considered as a self among other selves, but as an *apperceptionsmasse*. The child's relations to the other members of the group, to which he belongs, have no immediate bearing on the material nor on the learning of it. The banishment from the traditional school work of play and of any adult activities in which the child could have a part as a child, i.e., the banishment of processes in which the child can be conscious of himself in relation to others, means that the process of learning has as little social content as possible.

An explanation of the different attitudes in the training of the child in the primitive and in the modern civilized communities is found, in part, in the division of labor between the school on the one side, and the home and the shop or the farm on the other. The business of storing the mind with ideas, both materials and methods, has been assigned to the school. The task of organizing and socializing the self to which these materials and methods belong is left to the home and the industry or profession, to the playground, the street and society in general. A great deal of modern educational literature turns upon the fallacy of this division of labor. The earlier vogue of manual training and the domestic arts before the frank recognition of their relation to industrial training took place, was due in no small part to the attempt to introduce those interests of the child's into the field of his instruction which gathers about a socially constituted self, to admit the child's personality as a whole into the school.

I think we should be prepared to admit the implication of this educational movement—that however abstract the material is which is presented and however abstracted its ultimate use is from the immediate activities of the child, the situation implied in instruction and in the psychology of that instruction is a social situation; that it is impossible to fully interpret or control the process of instruction without recognizing the child as a self and viewing his conscious processes from the point of view of their relation in his consciousness to his self, among other selves.

In the first place, back of all instruction lies the relation of the child to the teacher and about it lie the relations of the child to the other children in the school-room and on the play-ground. It is, however, of interest to note that so far as the material of instruction is concerned an ideal situation has been conceived to be one in which the personality of the teacher disappears as completely as possible behind the process of learning. In the actual process of instruction the emphasis upon the relation of pupil and teacher in the consciousness of the child has been felt to be unfortunate. In like manner the instinctive social relations between the children in school hours is repressed. In the process of memorizing and reciting a lesson, or working out a problem in arithmetic a vivid consciousness of the personality of the teacher in his relationship to that of the child would imply either that the teacher was obliged to exercise discipline to carry on the process of instruction, and this must in the nature of the case constitute friction and division of attention, or else that the child's interest is distracted from the subject matter of the lesson, to something in which the personality of the teacher and pupil might find some other content; for even a teacher's approval and a child's delight therein has no essential relation to the mere subject matter of arithmetic or English. It certainly has no such relationship as that implied in apprenticeship, in the boy's helping on the farm or the girl's helping in the housekeeping, has no such relationship as that of members of an athletic team to each other. In these latter instances the vivid consciousness of the self of the child and of his master, of the parents whom he helps and of the associates with whom he plays is part of the child's consciousness of what he is doing, and his consciousness of these personal relationships involves no division of attention. Now it had been a part of the fallacy of an intellectualistic pedagogy that a divided attention was necessary to insure application of attention—that the rewards, and especially the punishments, of the school hung before the child's mind to catch the attention that was wandering from the task, and through their associations with the schoolwork to bring it back to the task. This involves a continual vibration of attention on the part of the average child between the task and the sanctions of school discipline. It is only the psychology of school discipline that is social. The pains and penalties, the pleasures of success in competition, of favorable mention of all sorts implies vivid self-consciousness. It is evident that advantage would follow from making the consciousness of self or selves which is the life of the child's play—on its competition or cooperation—have as essential a place in instruction. To use Professor Dewey's phrase, instruction should be an interchange of experience in which the child brings his experience to be interpreted by the experience of the parent or teacher. This recognizes that education is interchange of ideas, is conversation—belongs to a universe of discourse. If the lesson is simply set for the child—is not his own problem—the recognition of himself as facing a task and a task-master is no part of the solution of the problem. But a difficulty which the child feels and brings to his parent or teacher for solution is helped on toward interpretation by the consciousness of the child's relation to his pastors and masters. Just in so far as the subject matter of instruction can be brought into the form of problems arising in the experience of the child—just so far will the relation of the child to the instructor become a part of the natural solution of the problem—actual success of a teacher depends in large measure upon this capacity to state the subject matter of instruction in terms of the experience of the children. The recognition of the value of industrial and vocational training comes back at once to this, that what the child has to learn is what he wants to acquire, to become the man. Under these conditions instruction takes on frankly the form of conversation, as much sought by the pupil as the instructor.

I take it therefore to be a scientific task to which education should set itself that of making the subject matter of its instruction the material of personal intercourse between pupils and instructors, and between the children themselves. The substitution of the converse of concrete individuals for the pale abstractions of thought.

To a large extent our school organization reserves the use of the personal relation between teacher and taught for the negative side, for the prohibitions. The lack of interest in the personal content of the lesson is in fact startling when one considers that it is the personal form in which the instruction should be given. The best illustration of this lack of interest we find in the problems which disgrace our arithmetics. They are supposed matters of converse, but their content is so bare, their abstractions so raggedly covered with the form of questions about such marketing and shopping and building as never were on sea or land, that one sees that the social form of instruction is a form only for the writer of the arithmetic. When further we consider how utterly inadequate the teaching force of our public schools is to transform this matter into concrete experience of the children or even into their own experience, the hopelessness of the situation is overwhelming. Ostwald has written a text-book of chemistry for the secondary school which has done what every textbook should do. It is not only that the material shows real respect for the intelligence of the student, but it is so organized that the development of the subject matter is in reality the action and reaction of one mind upon another mind. The dictum of the Platonic Socrates, that one must follow the argument where it leads in the dialogue, should be the motto of the writer of text-books.

It has been indicated already that language being essentially social in its nature thinking with the child is rendered concrete by taking on the form of conversation. It has been also indicated that this can take place only when the thought has reference to a real problem in the experience of the child. The further demand for control over attention carries us back to the conditions of attention. Here again we find that traditional school practice depends upon social consciousness for bringing the wandering attention back to the task, when it finds that the subjective conditions of attention to the material of instruction are lacking, and even attempts to carry over a formal self-consciousness into attention, when through the sense of duty the pupil is called upon to identify the solution of the problem with himself. On the other hand, we have in vocational instruction the situation in which the student has identified his impulses with the subject matter of the task. In the former case, as in the case of instruction, our traditional practice makes use of the self-consciousness of the child in its least effective form. The material of the lesson is not identified with the impulses of the child. The attention is not due to the organization of impulses to outgoing activity. The organization of typical school attention is that of a school self, expressing subordination to school authority and identity of conduct with that of all the other children in the room. It is largely inhibitive—a consciousness of what one must not do, but the inhibitions do not arise out of the consciousness of what one is doing. It is the nature of school attention to abstract from the content of any specific task. The child must give attention *first* and *then* undertake any task which is assigned him, while normal attention is essentially selective and depends for its inhibitions upon the specific act.

Now consciousness of self should follow upon that of attention, and consists in a reference of the act, which attention has mediated, to the social self. It brings about a conscious organization of this particular act with the individual as a whole—makes it his act, and can only be effectively accomplished when the attention is an actual organization of impulses seeking expression. The separation between the self, implied in typical school attention, and the content of the school tasks, makes such an organization difficult if not impossible.

In a word attention is a process of organization of consciousness. It results in the reenforcement and inhibitions of perceptions and ideas. It is always a part of an act and involves the relation of that act to the whole field of consciousness. This relation to the whole field of consciousness finds its expression in consciousness of self. But the consciousness of self depends primarily upon social relations. The self arises in consciousness *pari passu* with the recognition and definition of other selves. It is therefore unfruitful if not impossible to attempt to scientifically control the attention of children in their formal education, unless they are regarded as social beings in dealing with the very material of instruction. It is this essentially social character of attention which gives its peculiar grip to vocational training. From the psychological point of view, not only the method and material but also the means of holding the pupils' attention must be socialized.

Finally a word may be added with reference to the evaluations —the emotional reactions—which our education should call forth. There is no phase of our public school training that is so defective as this. The school undertakes to acquaint the child with the ideas and methods which he is to use as a man. Shut up in the history, the geography, the language, and the number of our curricula should be the values that the country, and its human institutions, have; that beauty has in nature and art; and the values involved in the control over nature and social conditions.

The child in entering into his heritage of ideas and methods should have the emotional response which the boy has in a primitive community when he has been initiated into the mysteries and the social code of the group of which he has become a citizen. We have a few remainders of this emotional response, in the confirmation or conversion and entrance into the church, in the initiation into the fraternity, and in the passage from apprenticeship into the union. But the complexities of our social life, and the abstract intellectual character of the ideas which society uses have made it increasingly difficult to identify the attainment of the equipment of a man with the meaning of manhood and citizenship.

Conventional ceremonies at the end of the period of education will never accomplish this. And we have to further recognize that our education extends for many far beyond the adolescent period to which this emotional response naturally belongs. What our schools can give must be given through the social consciousness of the child as that consciousness develops. It is only as the child recognizes a social import in what he is learning and doing that moral education can be given.

I have sought to indicate that the process of schooling in its barest form can not be successfully studied by a scientific psychology unless that psychology is social, i.e., unless it recognizes that the processes of acquiring knowledge, of giving attention, of evaluating in emotional terms must be studied in their relation to selves in a social consciousness. So far as education is concerned, the child does not become social by learning. He must be social in order to learn.

4

Exhibit of the City Club Committee on Public Education*

THE EDUCATION COMMITTEE has three sub-committees. One deals with the use of schools as possible social centers, one with hygiene in the schools, and one with vocational work.

The exhibit which deals with the schools as possible social centers needs no explanation. It is a very eloquent exhibit, which shows the possibilities and results of this use of the schools.

Another part of the exhibit presents to those who examine it a statement of the very extensive work that is done by the physicians and nurses in the care of children in the schools. It shows the result of this work in the diminution of contagious diseases. At the bottom of this chart you will also find a statement which presents a real problem in the hygiene of the school, and that is divided authority between the janitor and the principal. Anyone who is familiar with the school situation knows that we are having very unhygienic conditions in our schools, solely because we have such a diffusion of authority there that nobody is responsible for those conditions.

VOCATIONAL WORK IN THE PUBLIC SCHOOLS

The third committee, that on vocational work, has attempted to present a very interesting situation that I do not think has come home to the people in Chicago. That is the break between the compulsory school law and the attendance of the children upon the elementary

* As originally published in the *City Club Bulletin*, V (1912), 9.

schools. The theory is, of course, that the child enters the first grade at the age of seven, and finishes at the age of fourteen, having completed his elementary education. But there are actually 43 per cent of the children who never get into the eighth grade, and 49 per cent who never complete the eighth grade. Therefore, half of our children in Chicago never get an elementary school training, which we have always regarded as essential to American citizenship. The fault is not necessarily with the compulsory law. It is evident that the school itself does not have the hold upon the children, when they have reached or approached the age of fourteen, that it ought to have. These charts represent this break, showing that the children often drop out of school at the sixth grade.

We must introduce the vocational motive into our education. We must make the vocation an essential part of the elementary school education. I hope that you will give some study to the figures on these three series of charts, for I think that they are very important to a real understanding of the situation. The term "retardation" is used in this connection—a somewhat unfortunate term. The term which we use is that of "over-age." A child who enters the eighth grade after the eighth period, or who fails to be promoted every year, is "over-age." With the increase of "retardation" or "over-age" in the school, you soon find a group of children who drop out as soon as they reach the limit of the compulsory attendance law. It is not the only instance in which a permissive law has become unwittingly a standard in the community. Very often in our communities we find that this permissive law which lets the children leave school at fourteen has left in the minds of the people the idea that education should stop at the age of fourteen.

5

Educational Aspects of Trade Schools*

W HAT I HAVE TO SAY THIS AFTERNOON is of a rather general
character, and a good deal of it looks toward the future. I
think however it is worth while that something of a general character
should be said in this matter of industrial education—trade schools—
from the point of view of labor, for there is no question that labor must
define its attitude toward industrial education. It is coming—it is coming
as surely as improvement in machinery has come and will continue to
come; it is coming, because it means greater economy, because it means
greater success in the work—and what means greater economy and
success is bound to appear and bound to maintain itself.

It is necessary, first, that labor should take an attitude with reference
to a change of this sort which is appearing and likely to advance
rapidly. You probably well know that in industrial education America
stands distinctly behind other countries. In Germany especially, in
France, and to some extent in England and other countries industrial
education has been undertaken and carried on, and that it has been
recognized that this education is of the greatest advantage to the
industry of these countries. Whatever its import may be for the labor
union, for organized labor, there is no question of its value to industry
as such. We are behind in this respect as we have been behind Germany,
for example, in the application of science in many ways to industry.
We are behind, but when we commence to catch up we will catch up
rapidly, just as in the introduction of better methods of manufacturing
in the years between 1876 and 1890 the changes that took place were

* As originally published in the *Union Labor Advocate*, VIII, No. 7 (1908),
19–20.

immense. Men who came to this country in 1876 in the interest of the steel industry from England were of the opinion at that time that it would be impossible for the United States to attempt competition in the steel industry on account of the out of date methods we employed. In a very short time after our manufacturers became aware of the need for change in machinery, they showed themselves not only able to make the change, but they evinced a ruthlessness in throwing away that which they had and putting in new machinery, which put them at the head of the industry.

There will be a similar movement in industrial education. It has proved its advantage to industry and the captains of industry will insist upon having it. So that we stand before a movement which has begun and will continue; and it is something of course that very intimately affects labor itself. Labor then must take an attitude with reference to industrial education. What I have to say bears more particularly upon the educational side of the question, and from that point of view I can do nothing but welcome its advent. If any of you are familiar with the educational movement, you know that what we are seeking is a way of introducing in some fashion into the schools the vital element of life. We have suffered from a discipline which applies simply to the schoolroom and is not the discipline of life; and the educator, especially the reform—the modern—educator, has been looking for some way of tapping the real life interest from the outside and carrying it into the schoolroom. You know that manual training, constructive industries of various sorts, have been introduced into the schools, not simply for the results of the immediate training itself but also because the exercise of that constructive activity is supposed to bring the child into a closer relationship with life on the outside. But none of the efforts which have been made in connection with constructive industry—a great many of which we have in the Chicago schools—has succeeded as educators wish them to succeed. We have not as yet attained the result which we get on the farm or in the shop.

I presume that any educator will admit that from the educational point of view the training a boy gets on the farm, assuming he is in the hands of intelligent parents, is an ideal type of education, because the boy knows what he is doing; he knows the relation of what he is doing to the end in view; because he feels the connection of that which he is doing with the life of the family. It is an ideal type of training. We know the same thing is true in the shop, so far as it goes, though I am not saying that it is adequate education. The boy in the shop learns with a rapidity out of all proportion to the rapidity with which the child learns in the school. Go into the University, and compare the work done by the student in the so-called Arts Department with

45

that done by the same student in the Law School or the Medical School, and you will find an enormous difference. The student never knows what it is to work until he feels the relation of what he is doing to what he will be doing hereafter, until he realizes that what he is doing today belongs to the life of the whole community. The same thing is true of the schools—the people's colleges—as in the university. From the educational point of view, the introduction of industrial education, of work in trade schools, is something which we must heartily welcome. The question then is not whether we will have industrial training—we are going to have it anyway. The question is how this is to be brought about and how regulated. The question is whether it is to come simply in the interests of manufacturers themselves, in the interests of industry, or whether it is to be looked at from the broader point of view, whether there is to be a policy in reference to it which will recognize the full import of it.

Industrial education means something more than efficiency in shops, something more than technically trained men. It means greater efficiency in the whole community, because if rightly brought in, we are going to have better educated men and women in the community. It is a question of greater efficiency throughout the whole community.

I can understand what opposition must at once arise in the minds of trade unionists to industrial education. The very fact that our captains of industry themselves want it—that the men who are opposed to trade unions are eager for it, points to the belief that they will be able to draw from the graduates of industrial schools people who would take the place of union laborers, and indicates that there is another question here. I have heard an account of a school conducted in Cincinnati in certain steel works there. Boys were selected from among those in the high school; out of five hundred, some seventy-five were selected. They were given one week in the shops, and then a week in the so-called University of Cincinnati where they were put at the studies bearing upon the shop-work. In this way it took them twice as long to do the work in the school as if they had simply entered the school and not done the work in the shops; but at the end of the time their standing was to the standing of those who had taken the regular course as 90 to 60. These boys had done very much better work than the boys who were simply taking the study course. I was told that the questions they brought into instruction almost puzzled the instructors themselves. They went beyond the theoretical points and brought in new points of view, and gave a grip to the work it had not had before.

Now, as I have said, here are means of instruction of the greatest advantage to the community pedagogically, but if the community does not introduce them the manufacturers themselves will establish their own schools. There are many manufacturers already in the country who are establishing trade-schools. They will not only be schools for men to replace union men, they will also be schools which will give a narrow training and there is no necessity of this training being narrow. These boys to whom I refer were trained of course specifically with reference to work which they were going to do, that of trained mechanics in the shops—in science, physics, chemistry, and especially mathematics. It would have been possible for this training to have been of a broader character; they could have taken up the history of the industry, the history of the machines they were making use of; there could have been given in connection with this work not only the specific training necessary for their technique, there could also have been given a liberal education; and if the work had been properly given, they would have been just as interested in this liberal education, in this interpretation, as in the mathematics and science essential to the technique.

The community then must take possession of this industrial training, this work in the trade schools, and use it for the good of the schools. It follows then that organized labor should demand that industrial education be welcomed, but that it should be made a part of our public school system, part of that system which we can reach by votes, part of that system which belongs to the body politic of which we are members; that it should not be possible that this method of education which is of so much value to the community should be left in the hands of manufacturers who are only immediately interested in the training of skilled men. For these manufacturers—or, I do not mean to say manufacturers—our method of industry, at the present time has cut us off from trained men. We have introduced machines into our manufactories, and those machines have to be tended; they are specialized machines and they have to be tended by specialized men, and the man who tends one of these machines becomes a part of the machine, and when the machine is thrown away the man is thrown away, for he has fitted himself into the machine until he has become nothing but a cog. The only morale that such a shop knows is that of speed—speeding up. The man is fitted into the machine so that he becomes a part of the machine, and is constantly pushed on to do more work along this specialized line. The result is that when the manufacturer, or manager, wishes to get hold of a foreman or mechanics, he cannot find one among his own workmen because these workmen have been so fitted to do specialized pieces of work that they are unwilling, even for higher wages, to take the responsibility of directing the work of others. That is the result of this type of work. A manufacturer in this city told me it was necessary for his concern to go out to the country shops where men had to have charge of the complete product in order to find men who could be made into foremen. Our system of industry has cut itself off from the sort of training that gives to them the mechanics they need, and they find they must educate these men in some other way, and what they will do is to introduce schools, unless the public conducts these schools. But these schools must be conducted by the public because it is of immense moment to the public and because the motive industrial training gives is something that is needful in the public school system.

There is another point to which I want to refer. You are undoubtedly familiar with the fact that in this country, in Berlin, Germany, and in London, investigations have been made to find out how many school children go without breakfasts and dinners. The mere gathering together of the children in the schools has made it necessary that the community should take some sort of position in regard to the standard of living of the children who come there. You cannot gather children together and insist upon their having well-lighted rooms, proper desks, etc., and then deal with children who are so hungry they cannot do the work. The mere logic of the situation forces you on, and you are obliged to say, these children must have a better standard of living than they have had in the past. The school just so far as it goes is a way of setting standards. The school of course is not simply the common school, the high school, it is part of a great system, taking in the university, and is an institution that standardizes our lives for us. To introduce industry into schools means that just so far the community is putting itself into the position where it will have to introduce standards for industry. It is of enormous importance that these industries should be introduced at a point where the community is obliged to say they must be hygienic. That is that they must be carried on intelligently, for that of course is the attitude of the school, of the university, that work is to be carried on intelligently. It is of very great importance that the community should take over into its hands the standardizing of industries in the school, and just so far as we introduce trade industries into our schools we are putting the community into the place where it will sooner or later have to pass upon the standards of life of those working in the industries.

These are the general considerations, and of course, they look toward the future. It will be a long time before our public schools will be able to make use of industries, but it is bound to come, and it is of the utmost importance that organized labor should take an intelligent attitude toward such a movement, for, as we are at the very inception of it in this country, we can take an intelligent attitude toward it. We can look the whole ground over. We can ask, what is the policy we ought to pursue? I devoutly hope that the intelligent men in the Labor movement will get together and think this thing over, talk it over, and formulate an intelligent program that will determine the attitude of organized labor toward industrial education and trade schools.

6

Industrial Education, the Working-Man, and the School*

T HE EDUCATION OF A WORKMAN has always been very close to his trade. The dependence of his training upon his trade is expressed in the word *apprenticeship*. The apprentice has been trained by helping under the direction of a master in the trade. If we go back far enough we find apprenticeship as a necessary introduction to every trade, and indeed the only introduction. The elementary school appeared in the first place to train the clerk and accountant. It was part of the apprenticeship of the commercial trades. In the seventeenth and eighteenth centuries the artisans and laborers were not taught to read, write, and figure. The extensive commercial activity, the constantly increasing use of money, and the growing importance of reading for political and social life, gradually carried the demand for control over the three R's throughout the whole laboring class; though it remained for America in the early decades of our republic to inaugurate the common school with universal education. Under these conditions, the master artisan was expected to allow his apprentices to attend the common schools, but there was little or no connection between the schooling and training in the trade.

The school taught the use of language and number. Apprenticeship taught the vocation. It was true that the exercise of the trade demanded reading, writing, and figuring, but the apprenticeship system simply left training in these to the school. The two vehicles of educa-

* As originally published in the *Elementary School Teacher*, IX (1908–1909), 337–46.

tion remained separate and influenced each other either indirectly or not at all.

This was partly due to the function of the common school in America. It opened the door to all avenues. Our democracy elected men to office who had no more than a common school education. It is not very long ago that boys left the common school to read law and medicine. In a country in which everything was open to everyone and the common school was the door to all opportunities, the relation of schooling to the work of the apprentice was lost in its relation to more ambitious callings. The common school has retained its stamp of the first step toward the learned professions and political preferment.

Thus the education of the workman has been and has remained divided into two parts, the formal training in the three R's and the apprenticeship to a trade. These two parts have not been parts of a whole. The schooling has remained formal, bookish, and literary in its interest. The apprenticeship has suffered severely in the change of modern industry, but even in its better days it did not awaken any interest in its own history, nor in its social conditions, nor in the technique of better methods. The schooling taken by itself was narrow and unpractical, the apprenticeship had no outlook and wakened no interest outside itself. The two did not reinforce and interpret each other. In a certain sense they ought to have been in the relation of theory and practice. The apprenticeship should have presented the problems which the school solved, and the interest in the solution of these problems should have made the work of school vivid and educative. But while it is easy to pick flaws in this training, its results were admirable especially in comparison with the training which children of today get who work with their hands.

Apprenticeship remains in many trades, especially in those under the control of organized labor. The interest of organized labor has been, however, very largely that of keeping down the number of skilled artisans to that which the trade can profitably absorb. Organized labor has not accepted the control over apprenticeship to make out of it a better education. Nor is there uniformity in the trades. In many the apprenticeship system has quite gone by the boards, in others it is not at all adequate. As a system of training skilled laborers the old system of apprenticeship has disappeared and no consistent new system has arisen to take its place. The cause of the changes is evident enough. It is the machine that has taken possession of the trades, has displaced the artisan, and has substituted for the artisan, who makes an entire article, a group of laborers who tend the machines.

The effect of this upon the training of the laborer has been most deplorable. The more the machine accomplishes the less the workman is called upon to use his brain, the less skill he is called upon to acquire. The economics of the factory, therefore, calls for a continual search for cheaper and therefore less skilled labor. The success of the modern type of wholesale manufacturer of inexpensive goods has depended upon the vast numbers of unskilled laborers. Women and children have been swept into the factories to displace the more expensive labor of men. We are accustomed to recognize that the sudden use of this type of factory production was made economically possible by the huge markets which steam transportation brought to the doors of the factory. The other determining factor, the surplus of unskilled labor that could be absorbed by the factory and the mine, we are not so conscious of. We are also very well aware of the nicety with which the inventor can adjust the machine to a product which the market demands. We are not so aware of the equal nicety with which the inventor adjusts his machine to the cheapness of labor.

The most serious handicap under which labor suffered with the opening of the modern period of factory industry was the lack of any connection between the training of its apprentices and the technique of the machine. The intelligence of the artisan who made the whole article made of him an admirable citizen of the older community. It was this intelligence very largely which made the success of our early democratic institutions. The apprenticeship system made practical, intelligent, self-reliant men, as well as good workmen who did not have to blush for the work of their hands. The training was not, however, adaptable. The very skill of the artisan stood in the way of his adapting himself to the new régime. The skilled artisan was no more but rather less valuable than the untrained man. And machines invented to exploit unskilled and unintelligent labor in so far fixed the condition of the workman that were thereafter to tend to these machines.

It is perhaps idle to speculate as to what the form of the machine, and the method of industry would have been if the laborer had had the training, the science, and the sort of skill which enabled the merchant, the manufacturer, and the engineer to make use of the advent of steam in manufacture and transportation; but we can recognize that invention has shown a suppleness in adapting itself to any kind of product or market, in using every sort of science and technique, and that there is every reason to believe that adaptable intelligence, skill that could be generalized and applied in various ways, if found at that period in the artisans, would have been a more profitable field for invention than the lack of intelligence and adaptability which our present machines are built to use and exploit.

A skill that can be adapted must be based upon some theory. The shop must be reinforced by the school. Such skill can turn from one form of manufacture to another, as the manufacturer himself can turn from sewing machines or steam locomotives to automobiles. Such dependence of the shop upon the school, of practice upon theory, we find in our most up to date apprenticeship schools. In those of the General Electric Company, of the New York Central Company, of the Houston, Stamwood, & Gamble Company at Cincinnati, the schooling represents by and large a half of the preparation. The apprentice must understand the technique that he acquires so that he can apply it with intelligence, and this means power to do many things, not one thing alone. It means the creation of intelligence rather than speed in the apprentice. These apprenticeship schools will not allow the foreman to hold the apprentice to a machine because he operates it with greater speed, i.e.: these schools recognize that the man must not be subordinated to the machine if he is to acquire the sort of skill they wish in these upper class workmen. The school and the shop must go hand in hand in modern artisanship. Their lack of connection in the old system spells the disappearance of the old-time system as the old-time artisan has disappeared. There can be no question that the modern artisan demands schooling if he is not to be a mere creature of the machine. He needs the mathematics and drawing out of which the machine has arisen. He must know the formulas which are expressed in the tools that they may be his tools and adapt them to his uses. He must be able to read the blue prints that are the language into which the engineer translates the formula to carry it over into bodily form. This sort of training is the only kind that will free the artisan. It is not until he can comprehend the machine as a tool that he will not be a part of it. Not that the employer desires in his high laborers ignorance. He is building up expensive schools because skill here is money in his pocket. The history of the technical schools at Fall River, Massachusetts, demonstrates that the employee, the employer, and the community all recognized the need of this training in the artisans who were to employ the high-grade machines.

It is in the economic struggle that organized labor fears the apprenticeship school. It has fought to keep down the number of apprentices in order that their wages might be kept up, and their working hours more occupied. Industry being organized on the basis of surplus labor supply, it is natural that labor should suspect the employer of aiming to bring about a surplus of skilled labor not only to make sudden increase in production possible, but to enable the employer to fight the labor union. That many employers have this in view is of course true.

However, as long as advance in wages means skill there will be an inevitable demand among laborers for industrial training. Correspondence schools are profiting by this demand at present, at the expense of the laborer. In the end it would be hopeless for labor to maintain its economic position by entrenching itself behind lack of skill. If the apprenticeship school is the best method of learning the trade it will be adopted. The restriction of the number of apprentices must arise in some other fashion, for with these schools, whether in the hands of employers or in our public-school systems, the numbers cannot be fixed by the labor unions, and skilled labor outside the union will be more dangerous than inside the organization. Inevitably the manner in which the commodity of skilled labor is to be controlled will be changed. It will be controlled because it is an economic waste to the country to have a surplus of labor. Our present industries adapt themselves to this surplus and of course exploit it, but this does not in any sense justify it nor make it permanent. Industry has adjusted itself to and exploited child labor. The remedy for this exploitation is not to be found in reducing the birth rate, and thus the number of children. The community itself, becoming intelligent, refuses to permit such economic and human waste as that involved in child labor. It must reject as decisively a system by which industry drops its adult labor into misery when for the time being it is not needed, to pick it up again at a reduced rate when there is a demand for increased production. The social control we demand will come through increase in intelligence, and the laboring class is the last class that can afford to restrict its own intelligence. In our present industrial evolution the race is to the technically equipped or to those who can command such equipment, and in a competitive society those who lack such equipment must be subject to exploitation.

The tremendous revolution brought about by the factory system, the machine, has found every group in society equipped with sufficient free intelligence to enable them to adapt themselves to the changes incident to the revolution. The investor, the producer, the middle man, the technical expert, the engineer, the banker, fitted in with no friction with the new order and have profited financially. The capital of the artisan alone has been lost. His capital is his acquired skill. If this is simply in the form of a fixed group of habits every change in the method of manufacturing will consign workmen to the human scrap-heap.

The financial disability of the laborer is that which is generally contrasted with the greater freedom of the capitalist or those who can accumulate a financial reserve. A revolution in industrial methods may annihilate the investment of the capitalist and even wipe out of existence the occupations of officers and employees. Still those whose incomes have permitted the accumulation of a reserve have an indefinitely better chance of getting upon their feet again, than have those whose incomes admit of no accumulation. There is room for them in which to move. They can seek opportunity at a distance. They can wait for it. They can prepare themselves for new and unaccustomed occupations, while the laborer whose income is swallowed up day by day in the necessary outgoes for his and his family's daily bread, must do anything or nothing as it presents itself, at the moment, at his own door. There is no reason to depreciate this disability of the day laborer. It only emphasizes the other disability which has been above presented; the disability of skill without adaptive intelligence. The man who knows why he does what he does, is better able to do something else. Intelligence, the ability to see the relation of means and end in conduct, is the fundamental form of freedom—"and the truth shall make you free." A laborer with acquired skill for which he has no theory, approaches the condition of the purely instinctive animal. He becomes helpless the moment he is out of the environment to which his habits are adapted.

To these general propositions, which may be summed up in the old adage that knowledge is power, a reply comes from our technical schools and our universities. It is said that only a select few can afford to know; that our life has become so complicated that it must be governed by the highly trained expert; that it is the age of the expert who dominates our industry as really as he does our medical practice. And there are social philosophers willing to accept this judgment and build their conceptions of the future of society upon it. We are, according to them, to pass from the control of the political and financial aristocracy to that of the technical expert. Only they will be able really to understand why anything is done in the growing complexities of our society, and they will rule. And the answer to this philosophy is that the expert does not and in human history has not ruled. He has served. His greatest effectiveness is found among those who are intelligent. The expert even in industry demands not blind obedience but intelligent co-operation, and the more intelligent the co-operation can be, the higher the efficiency of the expert. What is wanted in an ideal machine shop, where the tools are made to do certain work, is that the man who uses the tools should be able to criticize the tools. He should be able to go to the man who planned and made them and tell him how they work and where the test of use shows that they fail and need to be improved. If human intelligence consisted in the knowledge of fixed laws and methods the man who knew them would be king. It consists in the constant interaction of theory and practice. Theory is called in to tell us how to act, and what we do shows us where the theory was defective. As long as we have got to check up and reconstruct our theories, our plans, our models by their working, there is going to be as great need of intelligence in those who use the tools, who install the machinery and fit the pipes, as in those who think them out and make the blue prints. No one can estimate the loss which our industry suffers from the lack of trained intelligence among the workmen. The loss arising not simply from injuries and wear and tear due to ignorance, but from the suggestions of inventions that have not been made, from the opportunities for saving and for increased efficiency of equipment that have not been used can never be estimated. The exploitation of ignorance and misery which is involved in machines tended by the unintelligent, the children, the physically and mentally unfit represents losses none the less real because they are not recognized. Any process that adjusts itself to the lack of intelligence is in just so far wasteful—if it might be served by intelligence. If human invention has been able to make use of the ignorant and stupid, it certainly could have adjusted itself the more to those who were informed and skilful.

There is nothing more democratic than intelligence, because the higher the intelligence the more it demands of others for its own best exercise. It is true that intelligence may be used to manipulate brute matter, and brutalized men, and it may so adjust itself to this task that it conceives its function is to use the unintelligent. Those who possess it may conceive themselves an aristocratic class apart, but this only indicates their false and inadequate conceptions. When intelligence goes into action of any sort it demands all the intelligence it can find. It seeks comprehension in its agents; because it never can keep tab upon itself; it can never adjust itself and its constructions to their purposes without working with people who are in so far on a par with itself that they can judge the workings of the machinery and the execution of its plans.

This needs to be emphasized not only to make evident the importance to society of the widest possible spread of intelligence and the fact that industry can afford to pay for it, but especially to indicate the nature of the intelligence and the manner in which it should be acquired. It is the sort of intelligence that is close to its application. Its results are the criticism of methods and means as well as their use, and the suggestions of improvements and economies. This calls for an interest in theory just as far as that is involved in understanding what is being done. Many of our best mechanics get it without going to technological schools. They find out what they need to know and get the textbooks, the formulas, the tables that are necessary for this purpose. It is a result to which many a more ambitious education reduces itself in practice.

It is just the type of education which higher apprentice schools in this country and in Europe give to those whom they expect to be the élite of their workmen. It involves a knowledge of a whole process, if one is to comprehend any part of it. Thus in the approved apprentice school a boy may not be held to a single machine to merely gain speed. He must be familiar with all the machines. Mathematics and drawings are necessary for such a training, at least as far as the control over them helps one with his task. A large part of mathematics is a language in which one can best state his problem. If his work brings problems with it the workman must have the appropriate language in which to state them. It is also a language in which the results of the work of others can be conveyed in the form in which they will help toward the solution of the problems. The same thing can be said of the blue print. The competent workman must be able to read his tables, his formulas, his blue prints. It is fair to assume that any workman who has had the right training can reach this goal. It is important to notice that so much theory as this does more than make an expert workman in a definite calling. It also gives the skill he possesses adaptability and pliability. When he has met problems and has solved them in his own occupation he gains a confidence in his ability to solve the problem brought by a change of occupation. Theory after all is nothing but the consciousness of the way in which one adjusts his habits of working to meet new situations. The man who has never made such readjustments is discouraged at the mere presence of the new situation. The man who has done it, who has some acquaintance with the processes and technical expressions by which it is accomplished has his interest aroused by the new situation. The acquaintance with, and use of, so much of the theory of an occupation as the exercise of the man's own function in it calls for, means that his habits are not fixed, that the man has an adjustable nature. His chances of fitting into a new economic situation are a hundred times better than those of the man who has simply the facility of a single process. In the exigencies of the shop such a man can pass from one machine to another. His speed is not at first what it will be when his reactions become almost automatic, but the knowledge which he has of the whole process and the ability he has of stating the new and the old jobs in the same terms render him a vastly more valuable man than the workman who is nothing but a part of a single machine. The amount of training which an operative, a workman, in any trade should have is that which will acquaint him with all the processes of his trade, and so much theory of his trade which will enable him to understand the tools he uses and the manner in which they operate, that he may both

57

use the tool to the best advantage and be able to check up its efficiency and suggest the sort of changes and improvement that should in his judgment be made.

So much training a mechanic, a farmer, a mill operative, a plumber, every artisan should have. In the bill of rights which a modern man may draw up and present to the society which has produced and controls him, should appear the right to work both with intelligent comprehension of what he does, and with interest. For the latter one must see his product as a whole, he must know something of the relation of the different parts to the whole, and he must know enough of the language in which the problems of his trade are stated and solved to be able himself to criticize his own work and his own tools. This indicates also the manner in which this training should be acquired. The apprenticeship school in which school work and shop work balance each other, in which the school provides the method of stating and meeting the problems which arise in the shop, has become the modern system of apprenticeship. As we have seen, it is distinguished from the older apprenticeship system by its school, and from the later system by the organic relation between the school and the shop. The school work commands attention because shop problems appear there. And the shop becomes educative because its processes are comprehended and thought out. This educational method is ideal from the psychological point of view, for the acquirements of the school are demanded by the practical activities of the boy. This result has never been attained in other public or private schools. The training in these schools has been planned largely with reference to occupations which are not to be undertaken until the pupil has left school. Hence language and number have been dry formal studies meaning little or nothing to the child.

Some schools have attempted to meet this difficulty by introducing what have been called constructive activities in the school, so that the problems of the children might be real problems. The measurements of the boxes they were making should give them their arithmetical problems. In solving the problem they would also be learning what amount of lumber they would need and what lengths they would have to cut off, etc.

With this in view, very varied activities have been introduced in certain private schools. The results have not fully met the anticipations. The children's work has not felt the compulsion which apprenticeship offers. The actual products of the factory set not only problems but they carry with them a discipline that the apprentice accepts. They set the standard which becomes the boy's standard because he wishes to succeed in his calling. No task which the child sets to himself, and no task which the school sets as a school, has this meaning to the child. His own task makes no demand upon him that is bigger than himself and sets no standard that comes upon him with compelling power from the great world of which he wishes to be a part. No tasks of a school can be made to take hold upon the child as the training does which is to admit him to the rank of men. Even in college the students will not work as they will in the law and medical schools where they get their professional training.

In an industrial democracy the citizen must sufficiently understand the tools and the processes to comprehend and criticize the tool and its use. This is not only necessary for the technical efficiency of the industry. It is equally essential for the social control of the conditions of labor. At present the workmen undertake this by controlling labor as a commodity in the market. The artisan has lost the vantage-point of the medieval guild. Their control was over the product and the process. It is neither possible nor desirable to reproduce the medieval guild. It *is* possible and logical to make the workman's skill the basis of his social position and financial competence. Where labor appears only as a commodity, the unit being any man, the group of laborers can protect their wage only by protecting the weakest man. His wage must be theirs and it follows that their individual outputs must be his. On the other hand, the more highly skilled workmen tend to get out of the unions because on the one hand they do not need its protection and on the other their own earning power is restricted. Or the unions of the more highly skilled trades are able to pursue so different a policy in protecting their wage and hours of labor, that they lose touch with the unions of less skilled labor. This break emphasizes the attitude of the unions of the relatively unskilled trades. It is of the first importance that the working-men recognize that skill—developed intelligence—brings an entirely different factor into the economic situation, from that of the so-called supply and demand of a commodity. That other factor is described somewhat vaguely as the standard of life. It is recognized in the higher salaries of skilled employees—of professional men. When you demand skill you must make possible the conditions under which that skill can be obtained and exercised. Those conditions involve not simply technical training. Intelligence depends upon conditions of physical and social well-being. Every new demand for skill will inevitably carry with it the conditions under which that skill can be obtained. The manner in which a community responds to this obligation will be varied, and will appeal to many motives beside the economic interests.

There is no community in which a more conscious demand is being made for larger skill on the part of its workmen than Germany.

There is no community in which society has faced more definitely the necessity of raising the standard of life of its working classes. State insurance seeks to meet the unavoidable accidents and disabilities. Supervision of hygienic conditions undertakes to eliminate the evils to which economic inferiority exposes great masses of men. Universities and schools of every character aim to put the intelligence of the laborer upon the higher level demanded by the self-conscious industry of Germany. And Germany has but begun to recognize the consequences which will follow with unavoidable logic upon her demand that her laborers be adequately instructed. Society cannot demand intelligent workmen without accepting the policy of rendering the acquirement of such intelligence socially possible. What the laboring classes have to fear, at least for the immediate future, is that the demand for skill will be too restricted; that our community will conceive that it can fulfil its industrial functions with an élite of trained workmen and a proletariat of the ignorant and unskilled. If organized labor can raise its eyes for the moment beyond its immediate quarrels with its employers, it will recognize that its most strenuous efforts must be directed toward the widest possible industrial education, and that this demand must be made on behalf of all labor.

There remains the school itself. The apprenticeship system, as it has been worked out by the General Electric Company, is pedagogically and technically admirable. It is possible and probable that such schools will be multiplied among large concerns throughout the country. But even with such extension of the system the demand for this apprenticeship will not and cannot be met. Every laborer who is going into mechanical industry or into allied trades should have this training. It will be a training, if we may judge from the experience already gathered, which will accomplish its task of instruction as the public schools have never been able to fulfil theirs, for it will, under proper conditions, draw upon the interest of all professional training, and it will always have the discipline which contact with the actual process and product brings with it.

Such training cannot be confined to those whom our great industrial companies educate for their shops and designing rooms. It must be the demand of labor that this system of apprenticeship training be taken into the public schools. Manual-training high schools should become apprentice schools. But in this case the curriculum should be one so far liberalized that the history and geography of the trades connect the apprentice's skill with the social and physical conditions out of which it has sprung, and in which it at present exists. The curriculum should also contain the study of the social community into which the graduated apprentice will go. He should comprehend the central and state government not only, but the legal and administrative features of the city within which he is to labor. He should understand the laws that protect him as well as those which threaten him with pains and penalties. He must know to what officials he can appeal and he should have some comprehension of operation of the courts and the city council. He should know something of the conditions which control wages and their relation to the calling he expects to exercise. If his years and interests admit, such a course should be one in elementary sociology, such as are already to be found in French industrial secondary schools, in which the ideas of social obligations, the meaning of social standards, and the relations of man to the community can be discussed. What the child expects to do and what he expects to be provides adequate motive power for study and application. They provide also the natural center from which his relation to the past, in history, and to the present, in the study of society, can be brought within his field of interest and comprehension and through which he can form those fundamental conceptions of social rights and obligations which constitute our morality.

There remains, however, the still more difficult question of the elementary schools, where at the present time the vast majority of Americans get all their formal education. As has been indicated earlier the rest of the community have suffered because the curriculum of the elementary schools has been fashioned to meet the demands of a commercial class, and for those who expect to pursue literary and professional studies. The arithmetics do not present the type of problem that the average child meets when he leaves school. The histories instead of bearing on the occupation and phenomena with which the child is familiar, and toward which he is attracted, are hopelessly political. One would assume, from the study of our school histories, that politics is the only phase of human society that has a history. Geography is abstracted from the actual relations of industry and commerce which would give it meaning to the child living in a world that is given over to the production of wealth

How the elementary schools will finally adjust themselves to an education that faces toward the occupations which its pupils will enter, remains to be seen. It is, however, beyond question that the training on the farm and in the shop, even of the child who is not yet old enough to enter upon definite apprenticeship, indicates the direction toward which educational theory and practice must turn.

Two great facts stand out. One is that we are forced to reconstruct our whole apprenticeship training, and that when this is satisfactorily accomplished it will carry with it not only satisfactory technical training but a much broader and more liberal education than our schools at present can give to those who enter industrial occupations. The other is that apprenticeship provides an adequate and indeed almost the only adequate method of instructing children. When we recognize that this instruction need not be narrow nor unenlightened the objection to the application of the principle in our public schools finally disappears.

7

The Basis for a Parents' Association*

I CONFESS TO A FEELING of bewilderment when I attempt to state to myself the duties and privileges of a parents' association. I know that I am not alone in this feeling, although there have been parents' associations before this, and though two such organizations have been taken up into this one. For, however admirable these organizations have been, they have not yet succeeded in making plain to the plain parent the exact function of these bodies. This is not said by way of criticism of anybody. I am in much too humble a mind to be critical. I am merely trying to voice the ignorance which most of us would have to express if asked for a definite statement of the ground of our being here in the capacity of a parents' association.

This bewilderment, like Gaul, may be divided into three parts: first, that inspired by the old school; then, that due to this school; and, finally, that with which the child oppresses us, when we conscientiously try to face our responsibilities to him.

The school used to be a thing apart. It stood in an isolation that was guarded by traditions as old, many of them, as our modern world. Its business was to grind information into the child, and perfect him in the simple methods of dealing with words and figures. It had its own methods for doing this, that were directed by a class apart, which wanted no assistance from the home, provided the pedagogue was clothed with sufficient authority by the community. The school, however, stood for something else beside the three R's. It was an institution within which the child was to learn obedience to the sovereign state

* As originally published in the *Elementary School Teacher*, IX (1908–1909), 337–46.

that had placed him within the school and subjected him to the ferule of the teacher. It was the gateway to the power that came with knowledge, and the child's introduction to a social institution that stood outside of and transcended his home.

The parent's attitude to this institution was and remains today a very contradictory one. He cherishes it as the proudest heritage from his fathers, the characteristic thing in American society, that which educational commissions come over from the other side of the water to examine, and which seems such a very curious thing to them when they get the school under their eyes. As a general thing, the parent supports it generously out of his pocket, and supports it against the world, and even against his own children.

But on the other hand, he is a merciless critic. He abuses the school and its board and its teachers. Of course, a great deal of this curious combination of attitudes can be explained by the peculiarity of man's nature, that is constitutionally "agin" the government and all its works—the very government which he has helped to constitute, and for which he is willing to give his life. Psychologically, one is not apt to exaggerate the relief to the mind which is obtained by criticism, and a free people will be the last to surrender the right thereto. It stands to reason, furthermore, that an institution which, like the school, stands apart, with the sign displayed upon it "Hands Off," necessarily makes itself a mark for such criticism.

However, this critical attitude is something different from that which men hold toward their government. Criticism has become the method of government. Representative government by means of parties is nothing but a government by discussion, or by, what is the same thing, mutual criticism, in which Robert's rules take the place of the noble marquis's. But there is no organic place provided for the parent's criticism of the school. It is not subject to any rules, and is therefore wild and uncontrolled. The school is not governed by mutually destructive criticisms; it is merely harassed by it. It is governed by itself, in accordance with the tasks which it has undertaken. It is true that enormous advance has resulted from even this uncontrolled criticism, but the progress has taken place inside of the school, when it had to recognize a pressure that had become unavoidable. The public that made the criticism and was responsible for the change did not help to work out the change nor feel the responsibility of the criticism. With reference to the school, the parent has had the misfortune which belongs to a perpetual opposition—the misfortune of making continual attacks and never facing the responsibility of the reconstruction which the attacks imply. It is inevitable that the attitude of the parent under these circumstances should fall under these two contradictory heads: either that of support *contra mundum,* or that of uncontrolled, and frequently of unedifying, criticism. Experience has shown that changes take place when an unusually big row has taken place; and the moral is, if you want a change to take place, make your row big enough. It is not the particulars of your attack that count—they belong to the pedagogic experts; you won't be admitted to that discussion anyway, and your judgment would be thrown out of court if you were. Confine your efforts to making the present situation unendurable, and leave to the doctors and dominies the expert task of getting out of the difficulties that you have succeeded in creating. When there are two sides to the question, as there normally are, there result two rows on opposite sides. For example, we abuse the school for its arid methods and abstract subject-matter. "In the midst of a modern world it remains in a cloistered medievalism. Our children's minds are dried up. They come nowhere in the course into contact with reality. The school has become a great machine for grinding in the cheapest and most trivial parts of our culture, while the essential things are wholly omitted, not to mention the unnatural method of controlling the child's mind and conduct." When, in response to this popular demand, manual training, and cooking, and sewing, and clay-modeling are introduced, an opposing uproar is raised over the money spent on the "fads and frills" of education, and the three R's become at once the solid foundation upon which alone successful endeavor can be built, and the school the place where this must be laid.

From the standpoint of this public school, the duties of the parent are to provide children for the school and the means of conducting it. His privilege is that of the uncontrolled criticism of the daily press and the political campaign. It seems to me that the exercise of these duties and privileges is a somewhat bewildering program for a parents' association. It may be suggested that the parent may come in from this outside position with reference to the school, and that by means of a parents' association; that he may familiarize himself with the problems of the school, and speak as one having authority and not as the daily-press scribes. There are two things that occur to me to say to this. Most of us are not able or willing to make of ourselves pedagogical experts, who could speak with authority on the questions of curricula and school methods *per se.* We are fundamentally interested in our children's education and experiences in school, but that interest does not make pedagogical experts of us; nor is it possible nor desirable that it should. If the mere fact of intelligent and consecrated interest in our children's welfare in the school does not put us into any other relation to the school than that of a tax-paying electorate, if it can do no more than add acid to the ink when we write to the papers under the caption of "outraged parents," then there is no especial *raison d'être* for a parents' association. The second thing, I wish to say to this suggestion, is that it is only in part that the pedagogical expert decides such questions as manual training *versus* the fad and frill, the parents accomplish results in no small part by stirring up the political waters in which others besides themselves may fish. If a body of parents knew what they wanted in the average public school, they would stand a better chance of getting it by making a political organization of their association than by becoming pedagogical experts; and that would be as illegitimate as the other would be unpractical. To sum this up: if the intellectual life of the school is without connection with the home, the school's organization, its theory and practice, will be independent of the home, and the school's financial and political dependence upon the home does not make the proper basis for a parents' association.

The implication of what has been said is that the proper basis for a parents' association is the natural interest which people have in the life and development of their children. While this cannot be used to make pedagogical experts out of people, it is actually the basis for a great deal more than half of the average child's education. There is no need of repeating the commonplaces about the influence of the home upon the child. It is true that most of these commonplaces have to do with the heart rather than with the head. I have heard an educator maintain at some length that the character was to be formed in the home and that the intellect was to be trained in the school. Still it is getting to be increasingly difficult to distinguish between character and intellect, especially in their training, and the training of the mind in its narrower sense is felt to be generally dependent in no calculable degree upon the more intimate environment of the family. This training is not going to be directed by any conscious pedagogical theories, but it is going on, and is aiding or thwarting that which is taking place in the school all the time. What is wanted is a school in which, in some fashion, the social life of the home may be a part of the life of the school. The vital connection between the school and the home must be social. I do not mean that this relation should not be the ground for most serious thought; but that the home ought to be related to the school, in some real sense a part of it, simply because the children are members of each organization, not because the parents are politically responsible for the existence of the school, nor because they have educational theories.

There is another current conception of the connection between school and home which seems to be as unreal as the others are unpractical. The school may undertake to be the whole thing. It may be assumed that a judicious combination of sweet smiles and potted plants, and the homely arts of cooking, carpentering, serving luncheons, gardening, and sewing, can be used to provide, not only the means and lubricants for school work, but also an ideal home atmosphere. The home, then, should go to school along with the children, and get inspiration, and incidentally learn to carry on the work of the school in the house. In this case the home is, of course, the mother. There is no doubt that home and school have learned and will learn a great deal from each other, but this mutual helpfulness has not served in any way to deprive either of them of its individuality. Neither the school nor the home can sit at the feet of the other, and mere adventures of groups of parents into the school for purposes of observation and edification do not offer any essential reason for the existence of a parents' association.

The school to which we send our children has undertaken to leave the attitude of the institution apart, and to take the same view of the children which belongs to a normal home. While it must be more conscious of the methods that it uses in instruction than the home can well be, it hopes to recognize the intellect and interests of the children as they actually are. It has therefore abandoned the privilege of being a law unto itself, and, though its methods call for the pedagogical expert, its results are open to the criticism of the plain man. But it remains true, here as elsewhere, that criticism without responsibility is uncontrolled and unprofitable. And I am myself bewildered when I attempt to state what this responsibility is and how it is to be exercised.

I do not see how the school can accomplish what it undertakes, unless it has relations with the family, which is the habitat of the child; and yet, as the child advances from the kindergarten to the higher grades, the demands of the curriculum constantly increase, and the tendency to restrict the view of the school to the child's scholastic achievements grows. It becomes increasingly difficult to take into account the social environment of which the child is a part. As far as I can see, the school cannot go to the family. The home must go to the school. But we cannot go as scholars, nor yet as mere observers, if the relation between us and the school is to be a vital one. I do not know that the situation is made any easier by the fact that the problem is so far from solution from the standpoint of either the school or the home.

This brings up the third ground for bewilderment—the whole question of our duties to our children. I have, of course, no intention of adventuring upon this troubled sea. I merely wish to point out that the presence of our children in this school, and our presence as members of this parents' association, carry with them the privilege, and therefore the duty, of identifying ourselves with more of the life of our children. I take it that parents who send their children to a boarding school in some sense shift from their shoulders the responsibility for the immediate social environment of their children, and gain the advantage, which is sometimes a questionable one, of making the school and the home of the child one, and thus breaking down this middle wall of separation of which we have spoken. Now, if this school succeed, it must accomplish in a more normal fashion what the boarding school attempts. But we are unable to put the responsibility for the success solely upon the school. If we wish to keep our children at home, and wish further to have them go to school, and finally to have the whole life of the child all of a piece, as it is in a fashion in the boarding school, we have at least to relate ourselves as much to the work of the school as the home life of the boarding school does to its scholastic life. If this can be accomplished, I suppose that no one will deny that the result must be as much more admirable than that which is attained in the boarding school as the home is a more admirable place for the child than the boarding house.

Out of the vagueness of the situation so much seems to me sufficiently definite: that in the ultimate solution of the educational problem the home will have as essential a part as the school; that in working out the problem the school and the home stand upon the same level, each representing one phase in the child's whole life; that the common ground that they have between them is the social consciousness of the child, which this school undertakes to make the basis of its training, and which is the very content of the home life; that the relation between the parents and this school is not one that has to be manufactured, but one that needs only to be recognized and allowed to develop. It is, however, more difficult to recognize something that has in the past escaped us than to manufacture something out of whole cloth; for the recognition involves a change of attitude. It would be much simpler and easier to construct an artificial program of an interchange of civilities and mutual criticisms between the home and the school than it will be to make ourselves realize the common, everyday relations between the home and the school, which are taken for granted, and therefore ignored. There is, on the other side, an advantage in this fact that the relation already exists and does not have to be constructed. It makes very little difference with what we begin, and there is no necessary prescribed order for our continuance.

If, however, we are to realize and emphasize the common ground between the home and the school—the social consciousness of our children—we must be able to follow them into the school, and comprehend there what we feel we need of the methods and principles of the school; and we must have some organ by which we can react back upon the social life of the school. For these purposes the constitution provides for two committees—an educational committee and a home committee. It is the function of the first of these committees to enable the parent to follow his children into the school, without interfering with the school work, and to become acquainted with what is essential for his comprehension. It will be the function of the other committee to bring out and emphasize what is common and needs further development in the mutual life of the home and the school. There is a social committee, to take charge of the gatherings together of parents and teachers and children. There is a finance committee, that will enable us to put our hands to the wheel, if any specific occasion arises that commends itself to us. These are, however, all but organs which imply activities, but cannot create them. They are means which we may use, but they are not congressional committees whose reports we may receive and merely accept or reject. They are not there to report on conditions and make recommendations for our action. They are the simplest devices that could be presented to enable the home and the school to get together, and in the end to live the life that is common between them.

It has been indicated above that if this relationship actually exists between the home and the school, it makes no difference at what point or points we undertake to become conscious of it. I shall be excused, then, if I present without order some of the situations in which the home and the school are dealing with the same problems, and where, therefore, they should be conscious of their mutual activities in a common life.

The physical being of the child permits of no discriminations between life in one place and another. His health belongs to all his comings-in and goings-out. It is natural, then, that about children's diseases the home and the school should come closer together, or at least earlier together, than elsewhere. Mutual precautions against the spread of contagion, mutual conscientiousness in protecting the lives of others, can arise only when the connection between the house and the schoolhouse is made by interrelation that is even closer than postal-card reports. Day by day we learn more of the possible control which we might exercise, not only over the course of disease, but over its appearance at all. It is absolutely certain that the existence of a very large part, if not all, of contagious disease is due simply to the isolation in which certain parts of the community are able to encase themselves —isolated milk and tailoring industries, isolated transportation undertakings, isolated homes and isolated schools. The separation of the people and the mutuality of interests is the reverse side of the shield in every case of epidemics. From the standpoint of health the quickening of a common consciousness is the most important practical step that can possibly take place.

There is another phase of the matter of health which seems to me peculiarly fitted for consideration from the standpoint of the common life of the school and the home. I refer to the instruction which our children get, or do not get, upon the subject of reproduction, and the various experiences, ranging all the way from the healthful to the pathological, that are generally referred to as belonging to the age of puberty. In the large amount of discussion, necessary and unnecessary, upon this stage in children's development very little has been said upon the unnatural separation in the child's life between the home and that dominated by the school. I would venture to affirm that a cordial and intelligent common attitude and reaction to these questions by the home and the school would eliminate 99 per cent of the whole problem.

In the whole question of the relation of the child to those about him, and the morality that depends upon it, it is a contradiction in terms to assume that normal training can take place from any other standpoint than that of the common social life that belongs to both family and schoolroom. I can but refer to the large number of activities, which used to belong to the home, that played so large a part in real education of the child, and which now must be replaced in some way in the school. The picture of them is vividly drawn in Mr. Dewey's *School and Society*. I merely wish to point out that the readjustment cannot be made entirely in the school. It implies an interaction of the child's school and his society.

In closing, I wish to point out that this great and admirable building in which our children's school is housed presents opportunities for organizing the social life of not only the younger, but the older children, that I think we have hardly realized. Its gymnasium, its lunchroom, its art-rooms, make it conceivable that the building may become a center for the co-ordinating of the social life of the older children that presents so many difficulties. If we can gather the outside life of our children in a large degree about the school, and enter into intimate relations with it, the ground would be cleared for dealing with questions that are almost hopelessly baffling at present.

I have merely attempted to suggest a few points at which the recognition of the common ground between the home and the school must be of incalculable benefit to them both, and therefore to the child. I hope that, as concrete suggestions, they may give further content to my thesis that the basis for a parents' association must be found in the common social life of the school and the home.

8

*Moral Training in the Schools**

T HE GENERAL INTEREST IN MORAL TRAINING in the schools is widening and deepening. The very important volumes on *Moral Instruction and Training in the Schools,* which are reviewed in the present number, reflect this interest most intelligently, in an international inquiry. There are other indications of this interest which are more striking if less enlightening. We refer to the systems of moral instruction which pass under the names of "Fairchild and Brownlee Systems." These undertake to seize real moral situations in the experience of children, and by striking comment to educate the moral judgment. In the system which is identified with the name of Mr. Milton Fairchild, these situations are found to a large extent in sport or in the child's ambitions for success in later life. Photographs catch and vividly reproduce these crucial situations, and the comment of the lecturer aims to identify these highly exciting and absorbing situations with equally vivid moral judgments. The method has received wide approval and the host of names that cover the circulars imply that in the judgment of many of our clearest minded educators and thinkers a solution had been found for this problem of moral education in what have been termed these "moral nickel theaters." There can be no desire on the part of anyone to discourage an effort which certainly has abandoned the mere moral maxim, and attempts to make use of the child's own experience, to help him to form his own judgment, instead of trying to din the results of adult experience into the boy's mind in the form of ready-made judgments.

* As originally published in the *Elementary School Teacher,* IV (1908–1909), 327–28.

There is, however, an inadequacy in the presentation, which should be emphasized in the interest of the very purpose which has called out these schemes. This inadequacy lies in the fragmentary character of the situations which are seized by the lecturer and his camera. A situation in a baseball game must call out a whole social organization if it is to have the moral value desired. Why is it that American sport to so large an extent, even in our colleges, has led to lowering of morals instead of leading to a higher ethical level? In the English public schools and universities it is fair to claim a morally elevating influence for sport. In America this has not been the case. We have not succeeded and probably never will succeed in organizing the whole social life of the school on the basis of sport as is the case in England. When this is done the judgment of the school and its history and ambitions appear in the conduct of the boy.

No really moral consciousness will be aroused until the school and its ideals speak in the conduct of the boy on the athletic field. In America the school and its ideals call for success, and it is questionable whether we can ever succeed in identifying the school tradition with the ethics of sport. Our school instructors who must remain the principal personages in the school community are not part of the school games. The presence and character of athletic coaches are sufficient evidence that the ideals of Rugby and Harrow cannot be reproduced in the American school.

But eminent English educational opinion deplores the lack of civic consciousness in the intellectual and moral atmosphere of the English school, and here it is possible to obtain an organized school consciousness which shall be moral and moralizing. In approaching this problem it is of the first importance to recognize that it is only as the school becomes organized as a social whole, and as the child recognizes his conduct as a reflection or formulation of that society, will it be possible to have any moral training in our schools.

9

The Philosophical Basis of Ethics*

THE EVOLUTIONARY POINT OF VIEW has had more than one important result for philosophical thought. Not the least important among these has been the conception of the evolution of evolution. Not only can we trace in the history of thought the evolution of the conception of evolution, but we find ourselves with a consciousness which we conceive of as evolved; the contents and the forms of these contents can be looked upon as the products of development. Among these contents and forms are found the temporal and spatial qualities of things, of the world. The very time process as well as the space of the universe lies in experience which is itself presented as the result of an evolution that arises in and through spatial conditions, which is first and foremost a temporal process.

The peculiarity of this situation lies in the fact that the involution appears in the immediate findings of science. Our geological and biological sciences unhesitatingly present epochs antedating man in terms of man's consciousness, and biology and scientific psychology as unhesitatingly present that consciousness as an evolution within which all the distinctions must be explained by the same general laws as those which are appealed to to account for animal organs and functions. It is true that occasionally a scientist such as Poincaré recognizes that even the number system, as well as Euclidean space, is but a construction which has arisen and maintained itself because of its practical advantages, though we can draw no conclusions from these practical advantages to their metaphysical reality. If this position be

* As originally published in the *International Journal of Ethics,* XVIII (1908), 311–23.

generalized, there results the conception of an evolution within which the environment—that which our science has presented as a fixed datum in its physical nature—has been evolved as well as the form which has adapted itself to that environment; that the space within which evolution has taken place has arisen by the same laws; that the very time which makes an evolution presentable has arisen in like manner. Now, to a certain extent the conception of an evolution of environment as well as of the form has domesticated itself within our biological science. It has become evident that an environment can exist for a form only in so far as the environment answers to the susceptiblities of the organism; that the organism determines thus its own environment; that the effect of every adaptation is a new environment which must change with that which responds to it. The full recognition, however, that form and environment must be phases that answer to each other, character for character, appears in ethical theory.

In a certain sense this is found in the statement which genetic psychology makes of the development of the consciousness of the individual. Here there can be no evolution of the intelligence except in so far as the child's world answers to increased powers of conscious control. The world and the individual must keep pace with each other in the life history of the individual. But the child comes into a world which receives him as a child. The world of the adult from the point of view of descriptive psychology, is an independent environment within which the child and his world evolve. Within the field of ethics, on the other hand, the moral individual and his world cannot consistently be presented as themselves lying inside another moral field. The growth of moral consciousness must be coterminous with that of the moral situation. The moral life lies in the interaction of these two; the situation rises up in accusation of the moral personality which is unequal to it, and the personality rises to the situation only by a process which reconstructs the situation as profoundly as it reconstructs the self. No man has found moral power within himself except in so far as he has found a meaning in his world that answered to the new-found power, or discovered a deeper ethical meaning in his environment that did not reveal new capacities for activities within himself. Moral evolution takes place then as does that of the child; the moral personality and its world must arise *pari passu*, but, unlike the psychologist's statement of the development of the child, it does not lie inside a larger determining environment.

I am not ignorant of evolutionary ethics, nor that every type of ethical theory in these days has felt itself bound to interpret the development of moral consciousness in terms of custom and institutions. Thus we seem to postulate not only a community moral consciousness,

a moral world which determines the growth of the moral consciousness of the individual, but also we imply that this determining moral
environment goes back into a past that antedates moral consciousness
itself. From this point of view, morality, i.e., control by community
habit, has determined the development of individual moral consciousness as tyranically as the intellectual world has controlled the growth
of intelligence in the members of society. But this paradox disappears
when we recognize that this control by the community over its members
provides indeed the material out of which reflective moral consciousness
builds up its own situation, but cannot exist as a situation until the
moral consciousness of the individual constructs it.

It is another statement of the same thing that moral consciousness
is the most concrete consciousness—the most inclusive statement which
can be given of immediate experience. There is no phase of activity,
intellectual or physical, no type of inner experience, no presentation
of outer reality, which does not find its place within the moral judgment. There is nothing which may not be a condition or an element
of conduct, and moral consciousness reaches its climax in the estimation
of every possible content of the individual and his situation. There is
no other type of consciousness which must not abstract from other
phases to assure its own existence. One cannot carry out an acute
analysis and respond to the beauty of the object of analysis, one cannot
swell with emotion and dispassionately observe. But we place every
phase of our experience within the sweep of conscience; there is no
one of these phases of consciousness which has not its legitimate
function within the activity when viewed as moral. It is but a step
further to claim that the abstractions of science and the expressions
of the emotion and the direction of attention in perception and in-
ference must find their functions and hence their reason for existence,
in the act; and that morality inheres in the act alone, but in none of
these functions of the act (if I may be allowed two meanings of
function in the same sentence).

It is, of course, possible to make this a metaphysical doctrine. If
one finds reality in immediate experience and admits that the various
intellectual, æsthetic, and perceptual processes exist only as parts and
functions of an act which is the ultimate form of immediate experience, then the recognition of the ethical statement of this act as
its fullest statement would found metaphysics upon ethics. The
presentation of such a doctrine, however, would demand first of all a
discussion of the meaning of the terms "immediate experience," of
"reality," and the "cognitive state" that answers to it. I have no wish
to enter this debatable field, that is loosely defined by the term *pragmatism.*

There are, however, certain implications of modern ethical doctrine which fall within the lines which I have indicated above; that are of interest quite apart from their relation to metaphysical and logical speculations. The implications to which I refer are those that flow from evolutionary doctrine on the one side and from the identification of purposive activity with moral activity, and the recognition that our intelligence is through and through purposive. The first implication that flows from this position is that the fundamental necessity of moral action is simply the necessity of action at all; or stated in other terms, that the motive does not arise from the relations of antecedently given ends of activities, but rather that the motive is the recognition of the end as it arises in consciousness. The other implication is that the moral interpretation of our experience must be found within the experience itself.[1]

We are familiar with three ethical standpoints, that which finds in conscious control over action only the further development of conduct which has already unconsciously been determined by ends, that which finds conduct only where reflective thought is able to present a transcendental end, and that which recognizes conduct only where the individual and the environment—the situation—mutually determine each other. In the first case, moral necessity in conduct, for the conscious individual, is quite relative. It depends upon the degree of recognition which he reaches of the forces operating through him. Furthermore, the motive to act with reference to the end of the fullest life of the species is one which is primarily quite narrowly individualistic, and depends for a social interpretation upon the community of which the individual is a member. Moral necessity in conduct from this point of view is quite independent of the activity itself. So far from being the most fundamental reality it is a derivative by which, through what it is hard not to call a hocus pocus, the individual acts, for what is only indirectly his own—a distant end, through a social *dressur*. It is, of course, natural that this point of view should mediate the process of training by which men are to be led unwittingly to socially worthy action, rather than the immediate conduct of the individual who finds himself face to face with a moral problem. It is the standpoint of the publicist and the reformer of social institutions.

But if we admit that the evolutionary process consists in a mutual determination of the individual and his environment—not the determination of the individual by his environment, moral necessity in

[1] The full analysis of position assumed here has been given by Prof. John Dewey in his article, "The Logical Conditions of a Scientific Treatment of Morality," in Vol. III, of the Decennial Publications of the University of Chicago.

conduct is found in the very evolutionary situation. The possibility of intelligent action waits upon the determination of the conditions under which that action is to take place. The statement of these conditions becomes the end, when it is recognized that the statement is in terms of the activities that make up the personality of the individual. The content of the end is the mutuality of statement of personality, i.e., the tendencies to activity, in terms of the personalities who make up the environment, i.e., the conditions of the expression of the activities. It is because the man must recognize the public good in the exercise of his powers, and state the public good in terms of his own outgoing activities that his ends are moral. But it is not the public good which comes in from outside himself and lays a moral necessity upon him, nor is it a selfish propensity that drives him on to conduct.

It is inconceivable that such an outside end should have any but an extraneous position. It could never come into a personality except by the door of its own interest. The end could not be a social end. Nor could a purely individual propensity through the agency of community training become social. The moral necessity lies not in the end acting from without, nor in the push of inclination from within, but in the relation of the conditions of action to the impulses to action. The motive is neither a purely rational, external end, nor a private inclination, but the impulse presented in terms of its consequences over against the consequences of the other impulses. The impulse so conditioned, so interpreted becomes a motive to conduct. The moral necessity is that all activity which appears as impulse and environment should enter into the situation, and there is nothing which ensures this completeness of expression except the full interrelationship of the self and the situation. That one fully recognized the conflict which the impulse involves in its consequences with the consequences of all the other social processes that go to make him up, is the moral dictum. From the reconstructions that this recognition involves the immediate statement of the end appears. To enforce this dictum is simply to live as fully and consciously and as determinedly as possible.

The moral necessity for education is not an ideal of intelligence that lies before us of the clear refulgence of the intellect. It is the necessity of knowledge to do what is trying to be done, the dependence of the uninformed impulse upon means, method, and interpretation. The necessity of uprightness in public affairs does not rest upon a transcendental ideal of perfection of the self, nor upon the attainment of the possible sum of human happiness, but upon the economy and effectiveness, and consistency demanded in the industrial, commercial, social, and æsthetic activities of those that make up the community.

To push reform is to give expression to all these impulses and present them in their consequences over against those of all the other social impulses out of which an organism of personalities arises.

There is abroad a feeling of lack of moral force; we look before and after—to our ancestors, our posterity—for incentive to right conduct, when in fact there is no moral necessity which is not involved in the impulses to conduct themselves. To correct one abuse we must emphasize the interests it jeopardizes. There is no reservoir of moral power, except that which lies in the impulses behind these interests. To correct the sin of the individual is to awaken through the consequences of the sin the normal activities which are inhibited by the excess. It is this healthful, aggressive, moral attitude, which it seems to me is encouraged by the recognition that moral consciousness is the most concrete, the most inclusive of all. Here we must abstract from nothing, and here we cannot appeal from ourselves to a power without ourselves that makes for righteousness. In the fulness of immediate experience, with the consciousness that out of the struggle to act must arise all power to mediate action, lies salvation. In like manner evolution in moral conduct can appeal to no environment without to stamp itself upon the individual; nor to him to adapt himself to a fixed order of the universe, but environment as well as individual appears in immediate experience; the one coterminous with the other, and moral endeavor appears in the mutual determination of one by the other.

Nowhere is this point of view more needed than in the struggles which fill our industrial and commercial life. The individual is treated as if he were quite separable from his environment; and still more is the environment conceived as if it were quite independent of the individual. Both laborer and the society which employs him are exhorted to recognize their obligations to each other, while each continues to operate within its own narrow radius; and because the employer regards the labor union as a fixed external environment of his activity, and would have all the relations between laborer and employer determined by the method in which he bargains and does business, he becomes a narrow individualist; and because the laborer would determine these same relations by the methods which he has used in building up this union, he becomes a socialist. What will take that and other allied problems out of the vicious circles in which they are at present found, is the recognition that it is the incompleteness with which the different social interests are present that is responsible for the inadequacy of the moral judgments. If the community educated and housed its members properly, and protected machinery, food, market, and thoroughfares adequately, the problems at present vexing the industrial world would largely disappear. We resent the introduction of the standard of life into the question of the wages; and yet if the social activities involved in the conception of the standard of life were given full expression, the wage question would be nearly answered. Every such problem is the inevitable indication of what has been left undone, of impulses checked, or interest overlooked. We turn back to history and talk about the evolution of man as if his environment were not the projection of himself in the conditions of conduct, as if the fulfillment of the Law and the Prophets were not the realization of all that is in us. The sources of power lie in that which has been overlooked. Again and again we are surprised to find that the moral advance has not been along the straight line of the moral struggles in which a sin seemed to be faced by righteous effort, but by the appearance of a novel interest which has changed the whole nature of the problem. If we were willing to recognize that the environment which surrounds the moral self is but the statement of the conditions under which his different conflicting impulses may get their expression, we would perceive that the reorganization must come from a new point of view which comes to consciousness through the conflict. The environment must change *pari passu* with the consciousness. Moral advance consists not in adapting individual natures to the fixed realities of a moral universe, but in constantly reconstructing and recreating the world as the individuals evolve.

The second implication to which reference has been made, is that we must find the interpretation of moral consciousness within the act. The appeal to a moral order which transcends either metaphysically or temporally the moral situation; the besetting assumption of the moralist that a moral reconstruction can be made intelligible only by a perfect moral order from which we have departed, or toward which we are moving, have very grave practical consequences which it becomes us to consider. In the first place these assumptions rob our moral consciousness of the intellectual interest which belongs to them of right. If morality connotes merely conformity to a given order, our intellectual reaction is confined to the recognition of agreement and disagreement, beyond that the moral reaction can be only emotional and instinctive. There may be, indeed, intellectual processes involved in stating this moral order, but such statement is confined, in the nature of the case, to apologetic and speculative thought to thought which cannot be a part of the immediate moral consciousness.

A moral order to which we must conform can never be built up in thought in the presence of an exigency. There are only two types of reaction in a practical situation. One may respond to well-recognized cues by well-formed habits, or one may adapt and reconstruct his habits by new interpretation of the situation. In the first instance we have habitual conduct, in the second that type of reaction which has been most explicitly worked out by the natural sciences. Most of our action, of course, falls within the first category and involves no moral struggle. The second type, on the other hand, is that in which practically all our moral issues arise. If a practical scientific problem arises, such as the engineering problems in constructing railroads or driving tunnels, we recognize that the intellectual process by which the problem is solved cannot be a mere reference to a perfect model of conduct already in existence. On the contrary, just because the engineer is face to face with a real problem he must find in the physical situation facts of which he is at present ignorant, and at the same time readjust his habits in fact, it is the possible readjustment of the habit that directs his attention in investigating the situation, and, on the other hand, what is discovered serves to mediate the formation of the new habit. In a word, there is the typical play of attention back and forth between perception and response. In any such process the criterion which governs the whole and its two phases—three phases if we distinguish between perception of the new data and the formation of the hypotheses by which they are interpreted and mediated in the response—can never be external to the process. There exists as yet no plan of procedure which the engineer discovers or receives as a vision in the mount. The control is found in the relation of the different phases of the act which have been sketched above. It is the possibility of reaction to a stimulus that holds the reaction in the field of investigation and it is the continued investigation of the field of stimulus which keeps the reaction continuous and pertinent. The control is then that which was earlier referred to as the process of evolution in which individual and environment mutually determine each other. It is the criterion of action, which uses working hypotheses, but which cannot possibly be identified with an external ideal. This process, whether met in the field of mechanical invention, or the range of engineering, or that of scientific research, is recognized as the most absorbing, most interesting, most fascinating intellectually with which the mind of man can occupy itself, and this interest belongs legitimately to the solution of every moral problem, for the procedure is identical intellectually.

Yet we succeed in robbing our reflective moral consciousness of a great part of this interest. For there is and can be no interest in merely identifying certain types of conduct with those found in a given theory. For example, there is no intellectual interest involved in merely identifying the control exercised by a financier over an industry with the concept of property, and justifying him in doing what he will, within the limits of the law, with his own. There may be a very vigorous emotional reaction against the suggestion that he be interfered with in these vested rights; or, on the other hand, against an institution of property which permits such individualistic exploitation of social values, but there is no intellectual interest except that which is either apologetic or purely speculative. It does not come into the moral reaction to the situation. And yet the enormous content of interest which does attach to these moral questions is attested by the social sciences which have sprung up and expanded in every college and university.

It is interesting to compare the intellectual treatment which such problems receive at the hands of the scientific investigator and the pulpit. In the latter there is at present no apparatus for investigation. The pulpit is committed to a right and wrong which are unquestioned, and from its point of view unquestionable. Its function then is not the intellectual one of finding out what in the new situation is right, but in inspiring to a right conduct which is supposed to be so plain that he who runs may read. The result has been that in the great moral issues of recent industrial history, such as the child labor, woman's labor, protection of machinery, and a multitude more, the pulpit has been necessarily silent. It had not the means nor the technique for finding out what was the right thing to do. The science of hygiene threatens the universal issue of temperance, when we can look forward to the time when investigation may enable us to approach understandingly the prostitute and her trade, and change the social conditions which have made her possible instead of merely scourging an abstract sin.

The loss to the community from the elimination of the intellectual phase of moral conduct it would be difficult to overestimate and this loss is unavoidable as long as the interpretation of conduct lies outside the immediate experience, as long as we must refer to a moral order without, to intellectually present the morality of conduct.

In conclusion may I refer to another loss which moral conduct dependent upon an external ideal involves. The interpretation of sin and wrong with reference to a moral order external to the conduct fails to identify the moral defect with the situation out of which it springs and by whose reconstruction it may be eliminated. An illustration will at once indicate, I think, what I have in mind. The responsibility for death and accident upon our railroads cannot be laid at the doors of the system and those that work it, if an abstract doctrine of property and contract is used to judge the conduct of railroad managers and directors. The imperative necessity of the situation is that responsibility should be tested by the consequences of an act; that the moral judgment should find its criterion in the mutual determination of the individual and the situation. As it is, men who would risk their own lives to save a drowning man, regard themselves as justified in slaughtering others by the thousand to save money. Abstract valuations take the place of concrete valuations, and as the abstract external valuations are always the precipitations of earlier conduct, they are pretty uniformly inadequate.

But not only does an external moral ideal rob immediate moral conduct of its most important values, but it robs human nature of the most profound solace which can come to those who suffer—the knowledge that the loss and the suffering, with its subjective poignancy, has served to evaluate conduct, to determine what is and what is not worthwhile.

10

Scientific Method and the Moral Sciences*

I T HAD BECOME A COMMONPLACE OF THE PSYCHOLOGIST that there is a
structure in our experience which runs out beyond what we ordi-
narily term our consciousness; that this structure of idea determines to a
degree not generally recognized the very manner of our perception as
well as that of our thinking, and yet that the structure itself is generally
not in the focus of our attention and passes unnoticed in our thought
and perceiving. It was this dependence of our field of direct experience
upon such an unrecognized part of what we call mind that Freud has
made the theme of his doctrines, in a realm that lies on the border of
the abnormal or just over it. It is one of the valuable by-products of
the Freudian psychology that it has brought many people to recognize
that we do not only our thinking but also our perceiving with minds
that have already an organized structure which determines in no small
degree what the world of our immediate and reflective experience shall
be. It is possible to recognize other censors beside those dramatically
placed by Freud at the door of so-called consciousness to pass upon
the figures that enter our dreams.

It is to one of these that I wish to call attention. It is that the intelligible order of the world implies a determined moral order—and
for a moral order we may substitute a social order, for morality has
to do with the relations of intelligent beings with each other—and

* As originally published in the *International Journal of Ethics*, XXXIII
(1923), 229–47.

that this determined moral or social order is a world as it should be and will be. We may express this as Kant expressed it as a world in which happiness will be proportioned to worth, or as the Utilitarians expressed it by saying that it will be one in which there will be realized the greatest happiness of the greatest number, or we may give it more concreteness by looking to a New Jerusalem that religious doctrine pictures, or we may find it in a perfect Absolute of which we and our finite universe are but imperfect and inadequate parts and expressions. Whatever the conception of this moral order, definite or vague, it always has implied that the process of the universe in which we live in a real sense is akin to and favorable to the most admirable order in human society.

The most definite form which this belief or faith has taken in the western world is that of the plan of salvation as presented in Christian doctrine. The import of this doctrine was that whatever further purposes a divine providence might have in the conduct of the universe, man's moral regeneration and the growth of a society which this made possible was an end which was always involved in the physical world which was man's habitat. This was most succinctly expressed by St. Augustine, and passed into the form which is perhaps most familiar to us in Milton's "Paradise Lost" and "Paradise Regained." The sharpness of outline of the Plan has faded with the entirely new heavens and new earth which natural science, since the time of Galileo, has unfolded before men's eyes and minds, but the idea that the universe is in some way geared to the intelligence and excellence of our social and moral order has not disappeared from the back of men's minds. Scientists such as Huxley have pointed out the incongruities that lie between this conception and the findings of a physical science, that sees in the whole life of the human race but an inconsiderable moment on an inconsiderable speck within the physical universe, that finds in a civilized moral society an aberration from a biological nature that is red in tooth and claw, and subject to a ruthless law of the survival of the fittest. And yet men, even in moods which were not emotional nor mystical, have rarely regarded their habitat as hostile or indifferent to what was best in their social life and structure.

However, it is very evident that the aspect of this kinship between human society and its secular habitat which belongs to our present scientific age is and must be profoundly different from that of St. Augustine, or St. Thomas Aquinas, or Luther, or Milton. In no one respect is this perhaps more evident than in our attitude toward the evils which the catastrophes of nature, disease, and physical suffering entail upon us.

The view that the ordering of the world was primarily for the greater glory of God in the salvation of man, made of every event that affected men a direct action of providence with reference to the members of the human race, and there could be but one intelligent as well as but one pious attitude over against the action of providence, that of acceptance with thanksgiving or with resignation. Suffering and evil came as discipline.

It is hardly necessary to rehearse the steps in the development of the insistent curiosity of recent science, which has refused to accept any given order of nature as final, or to believe that seemingly inevitable events may not conceivably become quite different if we only comprehend what the manner of their happening is, or to forego the hope that human ingenuity may avert misfortunes if we can only understand their causes and conditions.

Here are two quite fundamentally opposed attitudes toward the kinship of the intelligence of men and the order of the world they live in. It is customary to call the one teleological and the other mechanical, to call the one spiritual and the other materialistic. The first attitude takes it pretty definitely for granted that we know what is right and what is wrong, that in certain definite respects we know what the social order should be; that the intelligent man in his moral conduct, and this is social conduct, starts off with certain truths given in his nature or by revelation, and shows his intelligence by shaping his action to these truths; that the path of righteousness is one that he who runs may read and a man though a fool need not err therein. If the moral order, of which these truths are an essential part, is given, then the kinship of men's intelligence to the order of the physical universe will show itself in the triumph of this moral or social order, and men can themselves start off with this order as a presupposition in their conduct in the world. The end is given in advance, this is the meaning of teleology, and if we are confident that the universe is so constituted as to achieve this end, we will be intelligent in acting on this assumption.

We have seen that Huxley quite frankly denies, in the name of science, any justification for this faith. He saw nothing in nature that was akin to the social or moral order. In fact he regarded what he called altruistic conduct as an abandonment of the road along which nature was going. This view of Huxley arose in part out of an interpretation of biological evolution that is seen to be inadequate. Kropotkin could point out that social organization, with just that sort of conduct which Huxley called altruistic, is as legitimately to be considered an outcome of an evolutionary process as is the survival of the fittest individual in the struggle for existence. But Huxley's position is of interest because it so ingenuously assumes that a moral order must be an order which is given in advance, while our knowledge of nature is all drawn

85

from what has happened. In our acquaintance with nature we can never assume a determining idea that fixes the result before it happens, as is the case when our ideas determine what the results of our conduct will be. So we speak of nature as mechanical or materialistic. This is just where the break seems to come between what we consider men's intelligence in moral and social conduct, and in men's understanding of nature. We can still believe, of course, that in the end the process of the universe will further ideals of a morally ordered society, and probably most men who are conversant with the findings of science and committed to its methods of research, still in the back of their minds, carry this faith, or attitude of mind, but this attitude can be of no service in understanding objects about us in the everyday life of the scientifically minded. It is reserved for religious moods, when we try to bring together what are in their logic incompatible.

Let us state this incompatibility in its simplest form. In our moral conduct we control our actions in considerable degree, i.e., in proportion as we are intelligent, by our purposes, by the ideas of results not yet attained, that is, our conduct is teleological. In our comprehension of nature the result is controlled entirely by antecedent causes, that is nature proceeds mechanically, and there seems to be no kinship between such a nature and the intelligence of men seeking for a better social order.

I have no intention of broaching the metaphysical problem of the relation of a mind that is spiritual and a nature that is material. The question that I want to ask is this: Can the world of natural science provide objects for the world of social and moral conduct?

If we drop back two or three centuries, whether we measure them historically or in present attitudes of mind, we find a view of the physical world which furnished the objects that purposive social and moral conduct demanded. In the first place the physical cosmos as a whole appeared simply as the stage on which the plans of a divine providence were being enacted. In the second place the separate objects with which men's conduct was engaged found their meaning in this providential plan and led to conduct which this plan for human society demanded. Men's attitudes toward disease, toward events which in present legal phraseology are denominated "acts of God," were those of supplication and resignation. In general those things which engaged human personal interest most acutely and which still had to be regarded from the standpoint of the community to which men belonged could always be conceived of as existing to fulfil the destinies of men in human society. In essence these physical things and occurrences were identical with their import for the success or failure of men's undertakings. They were as physical things and occurrences just what they meant for human conduct. Today a disease is the history of a bacillus, an earthquake is a shift in surface strata due to gravitational forces, while the incredible vastness of the spread of matter and its inconceivable temporal stretches in comparison with the inconsequential minuteness of humanity and its momentary duration rob the physical universe of any seeming relevancy to the fortunes of our race.

This is the more striking because the period within which this shift of cosmical values has taken place is that within which physical things and their forces have become subservient to men's purposes, to an extent that would have been beyond the imaginational stretch of the medieval or ancient world. The physical universe which by its enormity has crushed the human insect into disappearing insignificance has like a jinn in the Arabian tale shown itself infinitely complaisant in magnifying man's mechanical capacity. In accepting his negligible crevice in the physical whole man has found access to the minute structure of things and by this route has reached both the storehouse and powerhouse of nature. The heraldic device of man's conquering intelligence should be a design blending differential x, the bacillus, and the electron. If humanity has fled shivering from the starry spaces, it has become minutely at home in the interstices of the speck that it inhabits for an instant.

But if we have succeeded in applying science to our mechanical task, and in this have accomplished prodigies, we do not seem to have succeeded in applying scientific method to the formulation of our ends and purposes. Consider the Great War. The ideas that plunged Europe and then dragged the rest of the world into that catastrophe, the imperialisms, national, militaristic, and economic, are roughly identical with those that embroiled Christendom in the seventeenth century. It was only the weapons that crashed through those four years that belonged to the intellect of the twentieth century. There attaches to it the grotesquerie of a Yankee at the Court of King Arthur. Or consider the government of a cosmopolitan city, or of a great nation. There is at the disposal of the community for the carrying out of its policies the apparatus of a hundred sciences, but to secure the bare formulation of a policy we are forced to involve ourselves in the factional interests of parties that are psychologically closely parallel to the turbulent politics of an ancient or a medieval commonwealth. We are enormously clever at fashioning our means, but we are still in no small measure dependent for conceiving our ends upon outworn mental structures that our very science has invalidated.

But it would be a mistake to assume that scientific method is applicable only in the fashioning and selection of means, and may not be used where the problem involves conflicting social ends or values.

The advance of scientific medicine in dealing with public health amply substantiates this.

In this advance numerous social values embodied or championed by various institutions, government, the church, the school, and the family, have sought to maintain themselves against scientific procedure in combating disease and safeguarding health. Individual rights, religious dogmas and cults, family control of children, the economic advantage of cheap child labor for business, and many other accepted social values have been set up as absolute, across the path of progress of scientific public health conservation. But the demonstrated results of the hospital, vaccination, quarantine, and other means of medical service to the health of the community have forced men to bring these values into the field of other public goods and restate them so that public health could be the better preserved.

I imagine that the scientific advance of medicine presents as enlightening an illustration as could be found of the time that seems to exist between scientific method and our conduct in social and moral affairs. The human community did not wait for a medical science to convince it that health is a community good. Combating disease by its medicine men has been one of the chief common concerns even in primitive societies whose technique was entirely magical. We do not turn to scientific method to determine what is a common good, though we have learned to avail ourselves of it in some of our common efforts and practices in pursuit of the good. However, scientific method is not an agent foreign to the mind, that may be called in and dismissed at will. It is an integral part of human intelligence, and when it has once been set at work it can only be dismissed by dismissing the intelligence itself. Unfortunately men have committed this sin against their intelligence again and again. They have incontinently rejected the very method which human intelligence has learned to employ because its results came in conflict with other social goods which they were unwilling to either sacrifice or restate. But again and again when they have undertaken to use their minds thereafter, they have found that their minds had become committed to the method they had rejected. The past history of and the present struggle with venereal disease illustrate this, chapter for chapter. Scientific method does not undertake to say what the good is, but when it has been employed, it is uncompromising in its demand that that good is no less a good because the scientific pursuit of it brings us within the taboos of institutions that we have regarded as inviolable. Nor does scientific method assert that the family and the church are not goods because its pursuit of public health has trenched upon conceptions of them which men have held to be practically absolute. What scientific method does require, if it is to be consistently used, is that all the conflicting ends, the institutions and their hitherto inviolable values, be brought together and so restated and reconstructed that intelligent conduct may be possible, with reference to *all* of them. Scientific method requires this because it is nothing but a highly developed form of impartial intelligence.

Here, then, is the issue, so far as an issue exists, between scientific method and social and moral conduct. If the community is seeking an end by the intelligent method of science and in doing this runs counter to its habits in attaining and maintaining other ends, these ends are just as subject to restatement and reconstruction as are the means themselves. Nor does science pretend to say what this restatement or reconstruction must be. Its one insistent demand is that all the ends, all the valuable objects, institutions, and practices which are involved, must be taken into account. In other words, its attitude toward conflicting ends is the same as its attitude toward conflicting facts and theories in the field of research. It does not state what hypothesis must be adopted. It does insist that any acceptable hypothesis must take into account all the facts involved.

Now such a method can be in conflict with social conduct only if that conduct sets up certain ends, institutions and their values, which are to be considered as inviolable in the form in which they have been received and are now accepted. There is no issue between scientific method and moral and social conduct that springs from the fact that science deals with the relation of past facts to each other while conduct deals with future ends.

Science does not attempt to formulate the end which social and moral conduct ought to pursue, any more than it pretends to announce what hypothesis will be found by the research scientist to solve his problem. It only insists that the object of our conduct must take into account and do justice to all of the values that prove to be involved in the enterprise, just as it insists that every fact involved in the research problem must be taken into account in an acceptable hypothesis. Scientific method is at war with dogmatism whether it appears in doctrine, or cult, or in social practice. Scientific method is not teleological in the sense of setting up a final cause that should determine our action, but it is as categorical in insisting upon our considering all factors in problems of conduct, as it is in demanding the recognition of all of the data that constitute the research problem.

Scientific method does not insure the satisfactory solution of the problem of conduct, any more than it insures the construction of an adequate hypothesis for the research problem. It is restricted to formulating rigorously the conditions for the solution. And here appears a profound difference between the two situations, that of moral and social conduct, and that of so-called scientific research. In problems of conduct we must act, however inadequate our plan of action may be. The research problem may be left because of our inability to find a satisfactory hypothesis. Furthermore, there are many values involved in our problems of social conduct to which we feel that we are unable to do justice in their whole import, and yet when they are once envisaged they appear too precious to be ignored, so that in our action we do homage to them. We do not do justice to them. They constitute our ideals. They abide in our conduct as prophecies of the day in which we can do them the justice they claim. They take on the form of institutions that presuppose situations which we admit are not realized, but which *demand* realization.

Such an ideal is democracy written into our governmental institutions. It implies a social situation so highly organized that the import of a protective tariff, a minimum wage, or of a League of Nations, to all individuals in the community may be sufficiently evident to them all, to permit the formation of an intelligent public sentiment that will in the end pass decisively upon the issue before the country. This is what democratic government means, for the issue does not actually exist as such, until the members of the community realize something of what it means to them individually and collectively. There cannot be self-government until there can be an intelligent will expressed in the community, growing out of the intelligent attitudes of the individuals and groups in whose experience the community exists. Our institutions are in so far democratic that when a public sentiment is definitely formed and expressed it is authoritative. But an authoritative public sentiment upon a public issue is very infrequent. My guess is that the number of instances of that in the history of the United States of America could be told upon the fingers of two hands, perhaps upon the fingers of one hand. In the meantime, as the then President Taft assured us on an historic occasion, we are governed by minorities, and the relatively intelligent minorities are swayed by the import of the issue to these minorities.

However, we are unwilling to surrender the ideal of such a government, if only for the sake of the exceptional occasions upon which it is realized, but more profoundly because we cherish the hope that the form of the institution in some way helps toward the realization of what it promises. The most grandiose of these community ideals is that which lies behind the structure of what was called Christendom, and found its historic expression in the Sermon on the Mount, in the parable of the Good Samaritan, and in the Golden Rule. These affirm that the interests of all men are so identical, that the man who acts in the interest of his neighbors will act in his own interest. Actually the history of Christendom has been a history of war and strife, and we are forced to admit that in these dynastic, national, and civil wars has arisen the intensive consciousness of the larger communities. It was the horror of the Great War that aroused, perhaps for the first time in the human race, a public sentiment passing all national bounds and demanding some organization that could express this sentiment and avert a still more terrible horror. The history of Christianity is the history of men's refusal to surrender this ideal.

To indicate in what concrete ways, psychological, social, and technological, the presence of these ideals in men's minds may have directly or indirectly favored their realization lies beyond the scope of this paper. What must be indicated is that they have only been kept in men's minds by institutions set up for this specific purpose. An institution should arise and be kept alive by its own function, but in so far as it does not function, the ideal of it can be kept alive only by some cult, whose aim is not the functioning of the institution, but the continued presence of the idea of it in the minds of those that cherish it.

The church is the outstanding illustration of such an institution. Its most important function has been the preservation in the minds of the community of the faith in a social order which did not exist. At the other end of the scale may be placed certain economic institutions, notably that of exchange. The economic man may be an abstraction, but he certainly exists and functions, and we need no cult to keep alive the faith in the functioning of money, though there is hardly an agency that has had more profound effects in bringing all men into association with each other. Between these lie our various institutions. We feel from time to time the necessity of arousing in our souls an emotional appreciation of the value of the family, of democracy, of the common school, of the university, because in their actual operation they do not express that value adequately.

The psychological technique of maintaining such a cult is the presentation by the imagination of a social situation free from the obstacles which forbid the institution being what it should be, and we organize social occasions which in every way favor such a frame of mind. We gather together in a place of worship, where we meet on the single common basis of all being worshippers of one God, or gather at a Thanksgiving, where all the differences and indifferences of family life are ignored, or we turn with affectionate regard to the Little Red School House where all the children were found studying the same books and immersed in the same common school life. Now the emotional and intellectual attitude of these occasions is essentially different from that of any common undertaking to make the institution more effective, to reform it. The attitude implied in the cult of an institution is frankly hostile toward that which seeks its reform. The mental attitude attending a cult is always conservative, and if we are undertaking its reform we consider it reactionary. The emotional attitude in the cult of an institution flows from the very obstacles that defeat its proper functioning. We may become profoundly interested in the reform of an institution for better service, but if we wish to appraise it emotionally we envisage the wrongs, the vice, the ignorance, the selfishness, which the ideal of the institution condemns, and which frustrate its operation.

Now it is just these factors in social and moral conduct which render the application of scientific method, in that field, so profoundly different from its application in the field of the natural sciences. The formula is simple enough. Your conduct must take into account all of the values which are involved in the social or moral problem. But how are we to define these values? They ought to be defined by the conflict out of which the problem has arisen. In many cases they are sufficiently defined to enable us to act intelligently. If it is a question of visiting distant friends we find out how valuable it is to us, by the sacrifice of other things for which we wish to spend the money which the journey would cost. When we have counted up the cost, we may conclude that it isn't worth what we should have to forego. Of course the mere surrender of the contemplated visit is not the whole result. We have found out how much we want it, and have probably prepared to bring it about under more favorable conditions. For purposes of conduct, values define themselves definitely enough when they are brought into conflict with each other. So facts define themselves in scientific problems. The facts in the problem of the prevention of arteriosclerosis are the observations which indicate that none of the causes that have been supposed to conduce to it do actually account for it. The facts in the hunt for a pneumonia serum are that none of those constructed after the fashion of other successful sera give the desired immunity. The facts are determined by conflict.

But see how different the situation becomes when the problem is not the prevention of a disease, but the prevention of crime. If the problem were simply the determination of the values involved in terms of loss to the victims and to the community, over against the effort and expense involved in catching and punishing the criminal, the problem would not be a difficult one. No civilized community has ever hesitated to take these steps in view of the danger which the existence of crime entails. The difficulties arise over the methods of so-called criminal justice. It is supposed to prevent crime, but it does not prevent it.

At least it does not prevent it as vaccination prevents smallpox epidemics. It has some preventive effect. It is a palliative. But we cannot simply surrender criminal justice as inefficient, to use some other method, nor even to reform it simply from the standpoint of rendering it more efficient. For criminal justice has a cult value. We cherish the attitude of public reprobation of crime, or rather let us say of public vengeance upon the criminal, because of the emotional sanction it gives to a community ordered by a common law. We overlook the fact that we cannot keep up this emotional attitude without branding the criminal as an outcast, without in some sense preserving a criminal class or caste, and we are quite unwilling to estimate the value of this branding simply in terms of its preventive power. It has an absolute value too precious to be surrendered. If our social problem were simply that of prevention, we should have a standard by which we could fairly measure the values involved. We could never treat leprosy scientifically if we retained the older attitude of regarding the leper as unclean. The relatively recent history of the scientific treatment of the mentally diseased is one of passing out of a cult attitude toward the insane. Or consider nationalism. We cannot simply set about the elimination of war by methods which history has amply justified, because of the cult value of patriotism. The time-honored and simplest method of arousing the emotional consciousness of national unity is presentation of the common enemy. It is confessedly most difficult if not impossible to arouse this emotional consciousness out of the common life within the community itself. And at times patriotism seems to have an almost infinite value. The cult values are incommensurable.

And yet these problems are not only real problems, they are insistent problems, and as I have before observed, we cannot defer action with reference to them, although these and most of the other social moral problems are shot through with these incommensurable cult values. Nor can we take the attitude of the superior person, and affect the pose of one whose higher intelligence has raised himself above these incommensurables. They and what they represent are the most precious part of social heritage. But it is not their incommensurability that constitutes their value, nor should we hesitate to abandon the cult estimate of these institutions if their values can be stated in terms of their functions. The cult value of the institution is legitimate only when the social order for which it stands is hopelessly ideal. In so far as it approaches realization, its functional value must supersede its ideal value in our conduct.

It is to this task that a scientifically trained intelligence must insistently devote itself, that of stating, just as far as possible, our institutions, our social habits and customs, in terms of what they are to do, in terms of their functions. There are no absolute values. There are only values which, on account of incomplete social organization, we cannot as yet estimate, and in face of these the first enterprise should be to complete the organization if only in thought so that some rough sort of estimate in terms of the other values involved becomes conceivable. And there is only one field within which the estimation can be made, and that is within the actual problem. The field within which we can advance our theory of states is that of the effort to avert war. The advance in our doctrine of criminal justice will be found in the undertaking of intelligent crime prevention. The problems of social theory must be research problems. It is to one group of these problems which I wish particularly to refer. These are the problems of practical politics in the nation and especially in our municipalities.

I have already called attention to the chasm that separates the theory and practice of our democracy. The theory calls for the development of an intelligent public sentiment upon the issues before the community. In practice we depend not upon these to bring the voters to polls, but upon the spirit of party politics. The interest in the issues is so slight that any machine in a great city, that can insure by party organization and patronage a relatively small group of partisans who will always vote with the machine, can continue its hold on the city government for a considerable period no matter how corrupt its administration may be. It is perhaps this situation that leads us to overestimate the somewhat rough and clumsy method of registering public sentiment which the ballot box affords in a democracy. And in our heated efforts to reform corrupt administrations we accept the shibboleths of the professional politician that the essence of democracy is in voting on one side or the other. We attach a cult value to these somewhat crude methods of keeping a government of some sort going. The real hope of democracy, of course, lies in making the issues so immediate and practical that they can appear in the minds of the voter as his own problem. The wide spread of the manager instead of the manager or feed box form of city government is perhaps the most heartening sign of the times that this is beginning to take place. It does not seem to be an impossible task to get the average voter to see that the bulk of the administration of his municipality consists in carrying on a set of operations of vital importance to himself in an efficient businesslike fashion, that the question of public ownership of public utilities is simply a phase of this efficient administration, and that it is perfectly possible for a community to get such an efficient administration. The advance in the practice and theory of democracy depends upon the successful translation of questions of public policy into the immediate problems of the citizens. It is the intensive growth of social interrelations and intercommunications that alone renders possible the recognition by the individual of the import for his social life of the corporate activity of the whole community. The task of intelligence is to use this growing consciousness of interdependence to formulate the problems of all, in terms of the problem of every one. In so far as this can be accomplished cult values will pass over into functional values.

Finally I wish to recur to the dictum to which I referred at the opening of this paper: That the intelligible order of the world implies a moral or social order, i.e., a world as it should be and may be. What form does this take if we apply scientific method to social conduct?

We have seen that the earliest formulation of it by Christian theology was that the intelligence of the creator and ruler of the world must show itself in bringing about in this world or the next the perfect society which man's moral and social nature implied and that our intelligence consists in accepting the inspired statement of this order. Scientific method has no vision, given in the mount, of a perfected order of society, but it does carry with it the assumption that the intelligence which exhibits itself in the solution of problems in natural science is of the same character as that which we apply or should apply in dealing with our social and moral problems; that the intelligible order of the world is akin to its moral and social order because it is the same intelligence which enters into and controls the physical order and which deals with the problems of human society. Not only is man as an animal and as an inquirer into nature at home in the world, but the society of men is equally a part of the order of the universe. What is called for in the perfection of this society is the same intelligence which he uses in becoming more completely a part of his physical environment and so controlling that environment. It is this frank acceptance of human society as a part of the natural order that scientific method demands when it is applied to the solution of social problems, and with it comes the demand, that just as far as possible we substitute functional values for cult values in formulating and undertaking to solve our social problems.

The difference in the pictures of the universe presented by these two attitudes is striking enough. The one contemplates a physical world in which man and the society of men are but pilgrims and strangers, seeking an abiding city not made with hands, eternal in the heavens. The goal toward which all creation moves was to be attained through the individual members of the human community becoming good, i.e., living by certain absolute and incommensurable values housed and hallowed by social institutions. This morality or social *dressur* calls for only so much intelligence as is required to recognize these institutions and the claims which their ideals make upon us.

95

Anyone can be good, though but a few can be clever. There is hardly any kinship between this attitude and the age-long struggle of the human community to make itself intelligently at home in the physical habitat in which it finds itself. Man has domesticated the animals now these many centuries. He is but slowly advancing with painful effort in the domestication of the germ, though it is at present much more essential to community life.

The scientific attitude contemplates our physical habitat as primarily the environment of man who is the first cousin once removed of the arboreal anthropoid ape, but it views it as being transformed first through unreflective intelligence and then by reflective intelligence into the environment of a human society, the latest species to appear on the earth. This human society, made up of social individuals that are selves, has been intermittently and slowly digging itself in, burrowing into matter to get to the immediate environment of our cellular structure, and contracting distances and collapsing times to acquire the environment that a self-conscious society of men needs for its distinctive conduct. It is a great secular adventure, that has reached some measure of success, but is still far from accomplishment. The important character of this adventure is that society gets ahead, not by fastening its vision upon a clearly outlined distant goal, but by bringing about the immediate adjustment of itself to its surroundings, which the immediate problem demands. It is the only way in which it can proceed, for with every adjustment the environment has changed, and the society and its individuals have changed in like degree. By its own struggles with its insistent difficulties, the human mind is constantly emerging from one chrysalis after another into constantly new worlds which it could not possibly previse. But there is a heartening feature of this social or moral intelligence. It is entirely the same as the intelligence evidenced in the whole upward struggle of life on the earth, with this difference, that the human social animal has acquired a mind, and can bring to bear upon the problem his own past experiences and that of others, and can test the solution that arises in his conduct. He does not know what the solution will be, but he does know the method of the solution. We, none of us, know where we are going, but we do know that we are on the way.

The order of the universe that we live in *is* the moral order. It has become the moral order by becoming the self-conscious method of members of a human society. We are not pilgrims and strangers. We are at home in our own world, but it is not ours by inheritance but by conquest. The world that comes to us from the past possesses and controls us. We possess and control the world that we discover and invent. And this is the world of the moral order. It is a splendid adventure if we can rise to it.

11

Philanthropy from the Point of View of Ethics*

I N ITS CURRENT USE charity implies both an attitude and a type of conduct which may not be demanded of him who exercises it. Whatever the donor's inner obligation may be, the recipient on his side can make no claim upon it. Yet the inner obligation exists and in part limits the charity itself, for the donor cannot fail in his other commitments because he has answered the appeals of charity with too great a generosity. Within the appeal itself, however, lies a positive claim upon the donor which he recognizes, though he may be at a loss to estimate its force or to establish a criterion by which to judge between rival claims upon his bounty.

Back of the obligation of the donor lies the human impulse to help those in distress. It is an impulse which we can trace back to animals lower than man. There it is most evident in the parental care of the young, but the impulse may be called out by other relations. It may extend to adult members of the herd or pack to which the animal belongs. It is nicely interwoven with the hostile impulses in animal play. Its strength in humankind is at times deprecated by charity organizations, which desire to bring the impulse under rational control. The kindliness that expresses itself in charity is as fundamental an element in human nature as are any in our original endowment. The man without a generous impulse is abnormal and abhorrent.

Obligation arises only with choice: not only when impulses are in conflict with each other, but when within this conflict they are valued

* As originally published in *Intelligent Philanthropy*, ed. Faris, Lane, and Dodd (Chicago: University of Chicago Press, 1930), pp. 133–48.

in terms of their anticipated results. We act impulsively when the mere strength of the impulse decides; when the anticipated results of action either are not present in the volitional experience or do not affect the onward march of the impulse to its expression. We may condemn such impulsive action, but the condemnation is based upon the fact that a sense of values, with the consequent possibility of reasoned choice, did not play its proper part in the action.

It is evident that here is a field within which there may be no clear-cut moral judgments. How much influence should I allow to a dislike which I find that I have for an acquaintance? In certain situations this may be quite clear. I must pay what is due him. If the dislike is not justified by defects in character or ability, it should not influence my voting for him at an election. But I will not make him a companion on a journey or an associate in social undertakings in which temperamental agreement is of importance. Between these extremes there may lie a multitude of situations in which the impulsive attitude plays a questionable part in our decisions. Falling in love, and the conduct that grows out of it, are shot through with actions which are determined by impulses that are not and perhaps cannot be estimated in terms of consequences.

The kindly impulses that lead us to help those in distress lie within this field—so much so that they may breed beggars—while organized charity has arisen to bring reason into their exercise. Bringing reason into charity consists, on the one hand, in definitely tracing out the consequences of impulsive giving, and, on the other hand, of so marking out the distress and misery of the community that constructive remedial work may take the place of haphazard giving. Organized charity, however, covers but a small part of the field within which these kindly impulses express themselves. Among our own kith and kin, among our friends, in those undertakings that seek to advance human welfare and lessen its suffering in numberless ways, in "the little nameless unremembered acts of kindness and of love," these impulses are called out, and in few of them could we justify their exercise by a reasoned statement of consequences. Indeed, in many of them, such a rationalization of the impulse would diminish if not extinguish its worth and beauty. In kindness, the genuineness and strength of the impulse weigh heavily in our estimate of its worth and that of its author.

So far I have regarded these kindly impulses as if they stood upon the same moral level as hostility, sex, or hunger. And yet, in common parlance, kindness is nearly synonymous with goodness. That this is not merely a eulogistic approval of kindness by those that profit by it is evidenced by that sense of inner obligation which, as I have above indicated, is a part of our charitable attitudes. It is, of course, difficult if not impossible to isolate the fundamental impulses of our natures. Those which I have referred to as the kindly impulses are normally present to some degree however slight in our attitudes to all those about us; but the hostile impulse may quite completely banish them when it seeks the suffering and death of an enemy, and when our dislikes and resentments render us unsympathetic with their objects. In these situations we experience little or no impulse to assist them in their misfortunes, nor do our attitudes carry with them a sense of obligation to act as Good Samaritans. Nevertheless, the sense of obligation which is entailed by our social relations is present: economic relations obtain and persist; we must pay our debts and meet other obligations. In these economic and other social situations we do not simply respond to the stimuli which others embody—paying debts is not merely succumbing to pressure. We speak to ourselves, however unwillingly, with the voice of the creditor and of the community, assessing ourselves with the obligation. Our moral self-consciousness implies our own action as stimulus to our own response, and this action as stimulus appears in a comprehending assumption of the rôle of those who exact payment from us.

That the recognition of an obligation is at the same time the assertion of a right is tantamount to the individual's identifying himself with those who make the claim upon him. For an obligation is always a demand made by another or by others. When the obligation seems to involve only one's self or an impersonal landscape, the impulse to action assumes obligatory form only when the individual speaks to himself in the rôle of another. In obligation the values involved always assume a personal form. Thus in the expression of impulses in which those of kindliness are not dominant or from which they may seem to be entirely absent a man identifies himself sufficiently with the community to lay upon himself those obligations which he in turn exacts from others toward himself. In these situations, as I have said, the obligation does not attach to the impulse. The obligation lies in that response of the community to the individual's action with which he identifies himself. And it is these demands of others upon him with which he identifies himself that are the carriers of the values involved in the act. The impulse to strike or to help, for instance, is as yet unvalued. It is in the result that the value appears. When the impulses come into conflict with each other, the conflict announces itself in the incongruence of the ends which the impulses reach. One may not strike a man when he is down. And it is not the mere incongruence of the ends that carries with it the moral judgment. It is that voice of others in which we join that conveys the moral import of the conflicting values. Both must be there: the voice of the com-

99

munity and our own; the ordered community that endows us with its rights and its obligations, and ourselves that approve or dissent.

There is a definite movement within the field of organized charity toward the assessment of wealth for those purposes which organized charity seeks to fulfil. There is a certain amount of misery which the community should meet in its own interests as well as in the interests of those who are succored. A community chest presents a budget that appeals not simply to the charitable impulses, but to the sense of justice as well. In a word, charity carries a certain burden that ought in any case to be met. Those whose incomes include a surplus above the necessities, whether their souls are stirred by the suffering or not, may well recognize a responsibility to bear their part in meeting this community obligation. When this point has been reached there arises a logical demand that this should be met by the community in the same manner in which it meets its other obligations, through taxation.

Illustrations of this are found in compulsory insurance of employees against the disabilities of old age, sickness, and unemployment. In these situations the responsibility of the community for the disabilities, and the loss which the community suffers through them, takes them out of the field of charity. The appeal is no longer made to charity, but to the sense of justice. The obligation comes from the social values involved upon the individual as an integral part of the community. The morality of paying taxes for these purposes is in no sense lodged in a kindly impulse to relieve the misery which such systems of insurance undertake to meet. What I desire to maintain is that, when the charitable impulse does carry a sense of obligation with it, we always imply a desirable social order within which the goods which our charity confers would come to the recipients as their due or as part of their proper equipment for life in the community. It may be regarded as an unimportant truism to state that the moral standard of charity is to be found in the social value of the benefit to the recipient. In its commonest definition charity is doing good to others—especially to those who are most in need of it. But the ethics of charity is not exhausted by the recognition of the good that accrues to those who receive it. There is first of all the problem which I have already presented, the sense of obligation of the charitable person, even though that obligation cannot be enforced against him by society. The second problem is the standard which is implied in the appeals of different objects of charity.

The position stated above comes to this: that when a man feels not simply an impulse to assist another in distress, but also an obligation, he always implies a social order in which this distress would make a claim upon the community that could be morally enforced, as, for example, in a community where employees in industry are insured, the distresses incident to old age, sickness, and unemployment must be relieved. In contrast with this may be placed a conception that has obtained and still obtains in some circles, namely, that suffering and misery are part of the divine order, where they serve the purposes of punishment and discipline. Under this doctrine charity is a duty laid by God upon man for his own good, and which may accrue to him as a merit. I would still maintain that back of these legalistic conceptions has lain the assumption of the parable of the Good Samaritan that we are neighbors of those in distress; back of the eschatology of the church has always lain the thesis of the Sermon on the Mount that men are all brethren in one family. In immediate sympathy with distress we have already identified ourselves with its victims. In this the human kindly impulse stands above the impulse in lower animals from which it developed. In man even the immediate impulse that lies above the automatisms is the response of a self, and a self-experience is possible only in so far as the individual has already taken the attitude of the other. The very word "sympathy" announced this, as does the plea to "put yourself in his place," made in the effort to stimulate charity.

We characterize this sympathetic attitude of man as humane, as being human, thus distinguishing it from the impulse of the lower animal, for it involves participation in some sense in the suffering of the other. The participation exhibits itself in the experience of him who sympathizes, not so much in the sharing of the suffering as in the incipient attitudes of reaction against and withdrawal from the suffering object. We feel ourselves shrinking from or tending to push away the evil, and these attitudes stimulate our kindly impulse to relieve the sufferer. This is all, however, on the impulsive level. A sense of obligation has not yet arisen, for obligation arises only in the conflict of values. Even the immediate identification of the self with the other does not in itself take us beyond the impulsive attitude of relieving suffering. When, however, these values in terms of sympathetic identification with the others in distress are presented, they have a peculiar immediacy and poignancy; while, on the other hand, their very immediacy and poignancy militate against their statement in terms of rational means. It is difficult to carry over the interest in helping the immediate sufferer into long-distant plans for removing the social causes of the suffering. A man who is ready enough to put his hand into his pocket to assist a starving man who is out of work will hardly identify this impulse with a political campaign for insurance against unemployment.

These two situations present the *terminus a quo* and the *terminus ad quem* of reflective judgment in a certain field of charity. At first the act is hardly above the impulsive level—an almost unreflective push to relieve distress, the strength of which is largely dependent on the degree to which one "puts himself in other man's place," or the completeness of the sympathy aroused. This very attitude, however, of putting one's self in the other man's shoes brings with it not only the stimulus to assist him, but also a judgment upon that situation. Distress is conceivably remedial, or at the worst can be alleviated. The charitable response which we find in ourselves is one which can and should be called out in others, or more logically still the evil should so far as possible have been obviated. One cannot assume the rôle of the wretched without considering under what conditions the wretchedness can or may be avoided. As I have already indicated, the immediate effect of sympathetic identification with the other is to call out the other's response in attempting to ward off or alleviate suffering, and this calls out at once resentment or criticism against the individuals or institutions which may seem to be responsible for it. The step from this attitude to the idea of social conditions under which this evil would not exist is inevitable. Out of these ideas arise plans, possibly practical, for remedying at the source the misfortunes of those in distress.

This highly schematized path from impulsive charity to social reconstruction serves to indicate, on the one hand, a definite development which has taken place in many instances, and, on the other hand, that structural background of attitude and behavior which lies behind our humane impulses and out of which their ethics and philosophy arise. The very sympathetic identification with those we want to assist is in the logic of our nature the espousal of a cause. Universal religions have issued from their frustration—new Jerusalems where all tears are wiped away, Nirvanas where all wants have ceased. In any case it must be in our reactions against evils, and with its victims with whom we sympathize, that the ethics of charity must lie. The bare impulse to help is on the same level with that of the dogs that licked the sores on Lazarus' body. The identification of ourselves with Lazarus puts in motion those immediate defensive reactions which give rise not only to efforts of amelioration but also to judgments of value and plans for social reform.

It is a mistake, however, to assume that putting one's self in the place of the other is confined to the kindly or charitable attitude. Even in a hostile attack one feels in his own muscles the response of the other, but this only arouses still further one's own attack and directs the response to the attack of the opponent; and in the consciousness of one's rights one places himself in the attitude of others who acknowledge that right in so far as he recognizes this right as inhering in them. These identifications with others lead to self-assertion and a sense of individuality, which eventuate in the maintenance of self-interest and, at a further remove, in a sense of justice. They do not involve that sympathetic identification with the other which belongs to the kindly impulses. In the latter, one expresses himself in assistance and protection. In so far as the impulse is dominant, the interest of the other has become his own, which he now champions. That one champions the interests of others, with which he has identified himself, implies a social order within which the removal of these evils would make the same claim upon all that they make upon the charitable individual. It is in the feel of this implication that there inheres the sense of obligation which we experience in the presence of distress and disability, though the social order in which we find ourselves may make no explicit claim upon us to alleviate it. The feel of this obligation may be very vague, a mere affirmation that such misery ought not to be. It may be formulated in the belief in another world, a world to come, or in another golden age that lies behind.

In taking the attitude of the other who appeals to our sympathy, the conduct called out tends to maintain the other rather than the self. There is, then, a fundamental difference in the organization of this behavior from that which characterizes behavior either in the attitude of hostility or in the co-operative acts in which the responses of others determine our own. In the latter the interest may be said to lie in the structure and maintenance of the self through his comprehending participation in the other or others. The sympathetic identification with the individual in distress, however, calls out in us the incipient reactions of warding off, of defense, which the distress arouses in the sufferer, and these reactions become dominant in the response of the one who assists. He places himself in the service of the other. We speak of this attitude as that of the unselfishness or self-effacement of the charitable individual. But even this attitude of devotion to the interest of the other is not that of obligation, though it is likely to be so considered in an ethical doctrine which makes morality synonymous with self-sacrifice. The earliest appearance of the feel of obligation is found in the appraisal of the relief to the distressed person in terms of the donor's effort and expenditure. The good of the man with whom we sympathetically identify ourselves is greater than that which would arise if we expended the effort and means on the ends of a self that refused to respond to his extremity. What I give up is slight in comparison with his need. This is but an early stage in the development of the moral judgment, and in the case of the generous individual may appear rather as a defense of an act under strong impulse than as a motive to the act. But even in the immediacy of the situation that seemingly involves only the giver and the recipient, there is the implication of a community in which the good has a universal value—"which of them was neighbor to him that fell among thieves?" It is, however, an implication that can become explicit only when the social structure and the ideas behind it make it possible to regard the others as neighbors. The generalization of the prophetic message, its conception of the community as the children of Jehovah, made this possible. In the Greek city-state it was only in political and economic relations that the citizen could realize himself over against the others in the community. The generalization of these relations was indeed possible, but only in terms of a reason which could be the experience of a few, and a reason which defined and fixed existing relationships rather than obliterated them. With the decadence of the city-state and under the empire the philosopher, whether slave or emperor, could regard himself as a citizen of the world only so far as he had thought his way out of the structure of social relations, rather than by feeling his way into them.

The moralizing of the impulse to identify one's own interest with that of the other evidently depends upon making this attitude functional in the society in which the individual has reached his self-consciousness and whose structure is essential to the maintenance of his own self. Religion in its ecclesiastical organization may make a place for a particular group who have sold all that they had and have given it to the poor. Such ascetic groups are in a sense samples of the social order that should exist. On the other hand, their restriction to cloistered groups is a confession that the attitude cannot be made the principle of society in this world. And this fixation of the attitude leaves the charity of the layman outside of any program of social reconstruction. Its value is a personal one, an act of piety, an expression of other-worldliness, and the acquirement of merit; or it may be regarded as engendering and cultivating worthy traits of character, consideration for others, kindliness—in a word, humaneness. Over against a too legalistic or vengeful justice it appears as mercy. Then there remain the countless instances in which a sympathetic charity informed with wisdom may rescue others from social shipwreck, from suffering and distress, and help them to better social and physical conditions of life. It is in these instances that charity shines by its own light and becomes almost synonymous with goodness. Here are values which can be intelligently weighed against each other when they come into conflict, and within the social order as it exists reconstruction of the lives and fortunes of individuals can be accomplished. It is indeed in this remedial activity, this salvaging of otherwise unavoidable losses in the community as it is, this amelioration of the existence of the "poor whom ye have always with you," that we generally conceive of charity. It found its place in feudal conditions which have obtained socially long after feudalism was politically defunct. *Noblesse oblige* was a sense of some sort of responsibility for dependents. It was, in a way, institutionalized in chivalry. Because of the close genetic relation between the kindly impulses and the parental impulses it has always been peculiarly vivid in its response to the misfortunes of children.

And still the evils which charity has thus corrected or assuaged have been part of the order of society, and the obligation felt by the charitable did not arise from the duties which were inherent in that order. We return again to the implication of an order within this sense of obligation. The close relation which has existed between religion and charity, as we have seen, has given form to this implication; but human experience, especially in recent times, has abundantly proved that the implication lies in social attitudes, which religious doctrines have formulated but for which they are not responsible. If we undertake to give it its simplest and most immediate expression, it would take this form: that the need to which we respond is one which would be met if the intelligence which informs our social order and its institutions could reach the development which is implicit within them. That is, the moral appeal lying behind the obligation to charity is drawn not from the distress that is to be alleviated or the deficient goods which are to be supplied, but from the sort of conduct and experience and the sort of selves which society implies though it does not make them possible. For example, the moral appeal to charitable endowment of education lies not in the darkened minds of the uneducated but in the fact that there is a wealth of meaning in life and profound values which would interpret it to all members of the community if our social order gave to all the cultural background and the training which would bring out these hidden implications.

The compulsion of the appeal lies first in the location of these values in the relations of men to one another and to the nature that forms the environment of human society. Science, art, religion, and the techniques of living simply bring out, render serviceable and effective, these meanings and values. They are the realization of the wealth which belongs implicitly to all members of society. Cultured classes in some sense have an access to this wealth, which is denied to masses in the community whose social experiences and relationships, nevertheless, constitute this wealth. And, second, the means of furnishing this access to continuously wider groups is not found in simply enlarging the capacity and functions of institutions which already belong to social intercourse and control. The present order of society does not make enlargement of cultural means possible, and our immediate duties are formulated in terms of the order within which we live. Those who have advantages cannot share them with the rest of the community. This could only be possible in a community more highly organized, otherwise bred and trained. So far as this community is concerned, we can morally enjoy what from one standpoint is an exploitation of those whose submerged life has given us economic and spiritual wealth which our peculiar situations have enabled us to inherit. To sell all we have and give to the poor would not change this situation. But we feel the adventitious nature of our advantages, and still more do we feel that the intelligence which makes society possible carries within itself the demand for further development in order that the implications of life may be realized.

It is this feel for a social structure which is implicit in what is present that haunts the generous nature, and carries a sense of obligation which transcends any claim that his actual social order fastens upon him. It is an ideal world that lays the claim upon him, but it is an ideal world which grows out of this world and its undeniable implications.

It is possible to specify the claims of this ideal world in certain respects. A human being is a member of a community and is thereby an expression of its customs and the carrier of its values. These customs appear in the individual as habits, and the values appear as his goods, and these habits and goods come into conflict with each other. Out of the conflict arise in human social experience the meaning of things and the rational solution of the conflicts. The rational solution of the conflicts, however, calls for the reconstruction of both habits and values, and this involves transcending the order of the community. A hypothetically different order suggests itself and becomes the end in conduct. It is a social end and must appeal to others in the community. In logical terms there is established a universe of discourse which transcends the specific order within which the members of the community may, in a specific conflict, place themselves outside of the community order as it exists, and agree upon changed habits of action and a restatement of values. Rational procedure, therefore, sets up an order within which thought operates; that abstracts in varying degrees from the actual structure of society. It is a social order, for its function is a common action on the basis of commonly recognized conditions of conduct and common ends. Its claims are the claims of reason. It is a social order that includes any rational being who is or may be in any way implicated in the situation with which thought deals. It sets up an ideal world, not of substantive things but of proper method. Its claim is that all the conditions of conduct and all the values which are involved in the conflict must be taken into account in abstraction from the fixed forms of habits and goods which have clashed with each other. It is evident that a man cannot act as a rational member of society, except as he constitutes himself a member of this wider commonwealth of rational beings. But the ethical problem is always a specific one, and belongs only to those habits and values which have come into conflict with each other. About this problem lies the ordered community with its other standards and customs unimpaired, and the duties it prescribes unquestioned.

The claims of the ideal world are that the individual shall take into account all of the values which have been abstracted from their customary settings by the conflict and fashion his reconstruction in recognition of them all. Thus, the otherwise-unquestioned right of a man to expend his own wealth in his business, family, and personal interests comes into conflict with the needs of youths in impoverished classes for enlightened and adequate training. The claims of reason are that these values shall be regarded apart from their character as private property and the social restrictions which limit the development of children of poorer classes. Whatever he ultimately does, the charitable man feels it incumbent upon him to consider what could be accomplished with a portion of his wealth if it were devoted intelligently to increasing opportunities for education. So much money, in abstraction from the interests that seek it, would spell the enlightenment of many and a raised standard of public education. It is only by stepping into this field in which the possible accomplishments of this wealth can be impartially contemplated that the owner of the wealth feels himself able to decide to give or not to give.

It is clear, however, that reason would operate in a vacuum, unless these values of enlightenment—of science, aesthetic appreciation, and human associations—can take on forms which are freed from the social restrictions placed upon them by the groups which have possessed them. The phrase "republic of letters" has signified this freeing of culture from its class connotation. In a sense it constitutes an ideal world, which does not mean that these values exist in a world by themselves, but that the products of science, art, and human association can and should take on forms which would bring them within the province of any mind and nature able to respond to them. Now the claims of such ideal values lie not simply or primarily in the widening of the community that enjoys them, but in the superiority and efficiency of the science, art, and human relations which are so freed. It is not until science has become a discipline to which the research ability of any mind from any class in society can be attracted that it can become rigorously scientific, and it is not until its results can be so formulated that they must appeal to any enlightened mind that they can have universal value. Artistic creation and aesthetic appreciation must attain forms which have the same universality of objectivity; human relations should become such that their full social import interprets them. Reason is then a medium within which values may be brought into comparisons with each other, in abstraction from the situations within which they have come into conflict with each other; and within this impartial medium it becomes possible to reconstruct values and our conduct growing out of them.

Furthermore, certain of these values, such as those of science and art, have been given a form in which they become accessible to all minds with adequate training and social background. That is, they have been given a form which abstracts them from the restrictions which economic, feudal, and cultural class distinctions lay upon great numbers in the community. This sets up what may be called the "democratic ideal" of removing such restrictions. Now it is within this field that charity is so largely active, not in setting in motion great schemes of social reconstruction, but in bringing about or helping to bring about in specific cases just such a removal of restrictions; and, I take it, the obligation which the charitable individual feels is the demand that these restrictions should be removed. It is not a demand which society as it is now organized can enforce against him. It is a part of the growing consciousness that society is responsible for the ordering of its own processes and structure so that what are common goods in their very nature should be accessible to common enjoyment. We vaguely call it "progress." The charitable man sees and feels in an immediate situation the opportunity of an advance in this direction, and the opportunity may become a duty which he lays upon himself.

12

The Philosophies of Royce, James, and Dewey in Their American Setting*

T HAT PART OF NORTH AMERICA to which our forefathers came, the
Atlantic Coast from Maine to Florida, and that ever receding
frontier of which they progressively took possession, that frontier that
was at last arrested by the Pacific stretching from Washington to
southern California, this far-stretching country defines in geography and
history the community of the United States of America. But while
historical geography thus draws its boundaries and marks out the set
of its vast adventure, it does not define and exhibit the mind that was
formed within this American community and that informed and
shaped the course of that adventure.

It was a mind that brought with it from Europe habits already
formed of ecclesiastical and political self-government. The dominant
habits were those of Puritanism and the democracy of the town meeting.
The philosophy of the Puritanism is indicated in the phrase "thrift and
righteousness." Calvinism had found a place for business within its
spiritual economy. It could find the blessing of God in what the
medieval church had called usury. It opened the door to a capitalistic
régime. God had given men property and blessed them in its increase,
and punished the unprofitable steward by taking away even that which
he had. In England, the Puritans and their successors from whom
the American colonists came remained after the restoration a subordinate
part of the nation. The monarchy, parliament, and the courts, and

* As originally published in the *International Journal of Ethics*, XL (1930),
211–31.

the social hierarchy from which their functionaries were drawn, bore witness to old feudal habits that still controlled the national life, set the standards of conduct, gave form to social values, and furnished their emotional resonance. The culture of England's ruling class, sprung from an unbroken history, dominated the spiritual life of the community. When the colonies threw off their allegiance to the English crown and entered the family of independent nations, they had brought about a change which was even more profound than their political revolution. They had changed the character of the state which gave the former colonists their political consciousness. When they recognized themselves as citizens it was no longer as members of the English social hierarchy. For this they had substituted a political national structure which was a logical development of the town meeting. The state has never impressed itself upon the American citizen. It is nothing but the extension in representative form of the political habits of the town meeting. The caucus and the political boss stand so largely for its *modus operandi* that it commands little weight of in- herited respect. It was not until the national state became a practical necessity in the administration and distribution of public lands that it became an essential part of the political consciousness of the com- munity west of the Alleghenies. Then it could be appealed to for the development of roads, canals, and railways. Apart from these the pioneers continued to govern themselves in the fashion of town meetings. Any man was qualified for an office if he could secure the votes for his election. And the astonishing thing was that it worked so well. Thinly spread over a vast continent, this nexus of town meetings not only governed themselves in rough and ready fashion but organized states which were organic parts of the United States, and the fundamental reality of it in men's consciousness was baptized in blood. But the reality of it grew out of the solution of their problems. It was a union that had to be achieved, not one that could be brought out like an invisible writing in men's ancient inherited experience. The habit of self-government in local affairs was an inherited English method, but the creation of a national state out of these habits was purely American. Despite two revolutions English society had preserved the outward form of a state which symbolized its unity in the forms of feudal loyalties, while the power had been shifted to a Parliament within which the representatives of new groups were given a voice in governmental control. But these representatives belonged to a hereditary ruling class who fused their representation of a rising democracy with the historical traditions of the English gentleman—the essence of English liberalism. Within the community the men whom commerce and industry had clothed with new demands placed these demands in the keeping of those who had the historic tradition and training. So the as yet un-franchised voters and the nonconformists could find their articulate spokesman in so typical an English gentleman and so vivid a church-man as Gladstone. The education and social training which we call culture was in the minds of Englishmen an essential part of the consciousness of the state. Carlyle wanted to deepen it into a religion and Disraeli saw in it not only the opportunity of Tory democracy but of a far-flung imperialism. The state could be realized not only in the symbolic person of the monarch but also in the dependence of the masses upon those whose training and social position gifted their representatives with the right to fight their battles within the ancient structure of the state. It was not only the military victories of England that were won on the fields of her public schools. The historical and functional universality of the state could be still incarnated in a social feudal structure. The training, the culture, and the ideas of its upper classes were essential factors even in the political struggles which democratized its government.

It is, I think, necessary to recall this fundamental difference between the American and English communities, if we are to understand the part played in our life by a culture which in one sense is as much English as American.

These differences of attitude in the corresponding groups in the English and American communities stand out most sharply, if we recognize that in England they were dominant elements in the middle class which was fighting its way to a controlling political position, a middle class which stood between a lower class of tenants, farm laborers, and the industrial proletariat of the manufacturing cities, on the one side, and the upper class of gentility, nobility, and the crown above them, on the other. In American society there was nothing below them and nothing above them. They did not have to convince a community of ancient tradition that their control would not sacrifice the values woven into its social structure and hallowed by its history. If the American Puritan was freed from the opposition of his English fellow, he was freed also from the necessity of deepening his philosophy to meet the demands of a more varied community. He had problems enough, but these did not include that of justifying his way of life and the principles underlying his view of the world to powerful hostile parts of his own community. This type of English individualism was set free to propagate itself in a great continent without its natural enemies.

It was an individualism which placed the soul over against his Maker, the pioneer over against society, and the economic man over against his market. The relations were largely contractual. Behind it lay a simplified religious philosophy, a theology, in which dogmatic answers were given to questionings as to the purpose of the world, the future of the human soul, moral obligations, and social institutions. Its Calvinism had separated church and state. It had come to terms with the Newtonian revolution and eighteenth-century enlightenment. Popular education and economic opportunity sprang naturally from its social attitude and its geographical situation. It was the distillation of the democracy inherent in Calvinism and the Industrial Revolution at liberty to expand and proliferate for a century without the social problems which beset it in Europe. The American pioneer was spiritually stripped for the material conquest of a continent and the formation of a democratic community.

It has not been, therefore, either in the fields of philosophic reflection and aesthetic appreciation or in that of historic retrospect that the American has sought for the import of his political activity. His most comprehensive institutions of social control and organization have found their reason for existence in the immediate problems of the community. The same is true of the economic life of the community. Success in business has not meant entrance into time-honored ruling classes. In no country in the world has striking success in business been so occupied with the economic organization and development in the economic processes themselves. Those larger communities which political and economic activities have always implied and involved, and which the historic relations of members of the European nations have in some sort expressed, have had little or no existence in the retrospect and historic structure of the American mind, with which to dignify and build out the import of activities which transcend their immediate field.

It has followed that the values of these social processes have been found in the achievements they have immediately secured or in the interest in the activities themselves, and as the immediate ends in politics and business are inadequate expressions of their values in the community the ideal phase of politics and business has been found in the process rather than in their objectives. This implicit philosophy has been inarticulate. That it is there is evidenced in the social values which have permeated and controlled political and economic life in America, values which have transcended our politics and our business. The advance which has been achieved in our society has in the main been due neither to leadership nor to ideas. There have been a few outstanding exceptions, but by and large I think this is true of the history of the community, of the United States. And yet we have inherited the literature, the philosophy, and the art of the Europe from which we separated ourselves in our political and economic undertakings. It was a culture which did not root in the active life of the community. The colleges which were the natural habitats of this culture, which should therefore have endowed with this culture those who were going out into the active life of the community, were not the centers from which the politicians and business men of the community were drawn. In the earlier years of our history they trained a larger percentage of the clergymen than of any other calling, but the separation of church and state was too profound not only in our institutions but also in our social attitudes to allow the church to be a dominant force in the direction of the onward life of the community.

It is this break between the culture and the directive forces in the community that was characteristic of the century and a quarter of the history of the mind of America. It stands out in all expressions of this culture, but it is to its import in philosophy that I wish to draw attention.

In eighteenth century thought, science had discovered laws in nature and assumed them to exist in social processes. As God enacted them in nature, let the monarch enact them in society; and personal obligation to these monarchs would insure their operation in church and state. It was the undertaking of the romantic philosophies to fuse these two principles of social control into one. Nature was rational and society was rational. The principle of control was reason, but this controlling reason could be found only in an inclusive self that contained nature and society. Contrariety, the irrational, contradiction, evil, and sin, in nature and men, could only be overcome by the wider experience within which these disappear in the rational. What the romantic philosophy undertook was to find this process, in which the contradictions disappear in the higher synthesis, within the experience of the individual mind; but as the solution must be already achieved in the timeless process of the infinite, the finite mind could find no direction for its conduct within its own reason. It could only realize itself in taking its place within so much of the transcendent whole as was evident in its experience. As that experience widened we could realize more and more of that infinite whole, but we had no such intelligent process within ourselves as would enable us to take the helm into our own hands and direct the course of our own conduct, either in thought or action. Still it was a romantic philosophy that was warm with the inner life of the self, and it vivified the past by reliving it. It brought romance into history and philosophy.

This romantic philosophy was reflected in America in Emerson and the members of the Concord School, but in America it answered neither to the program of the Absolute Idealists that sought to sweep all activities of the spirit, scientific, aesthetic, religious, and political, within the logic of the development of the self, nor to the undertaking of Carlyle to find within the depths of the self a principle of feudal leadership that could guide English society out of the wastes of the Industrial Revolution. It was allied in America to the clerical revolt against Calvinism and brought with it a romantic discovery of a self that could interpret nature and history by identifying itself with their processes, but it was worked out neither in the logic of thought and social organization nor with regard to the demands of immediate social problems. It was a part of American culture, a culture which was fundamentally European. But the American became self-conscious in his belief that he had broken with the structure of European society. He felt himself to be hostile to the society from which his culture sprang. Nor was this break between culture and social activities mended by the literature of the New England group. This was shot through with a nostalgia for the richer and profounder spiritual experience across the Atlantic. It followed from this situation that culture in America was not an interpretation of American life. And yet the need for interpretation was present in American consciousness, and the lack of a competent native culture was recognized. I believe that there is no more striking character of American consciousness than this division between the two great currents of activity, those of politics and business on the one side, and the history, literature, and speculation which should interpret them on the other.

This culture appeared then in the curriculums of American schools and colleges. There was no other to put in its place. America's native culture accepted the forms and standards of European culture, was frankly imitative. It was confessedly inferior, not different. It was not indigenous. The cultivated American was a tourist even if he never left American shores. When the American felt the inadequacy of the philosophy and art native to the Puritan tradition, his revolt took him abroad in spirit if not in person, but he was still at home for he was an exponent of the only culture the community possessed.

When the great speculative mind of Josiah Royce appeared in a California mining camp and faced the problem of good and evil and examined the current judgments and the presuppositions back of them, he inevitably turned to the great philosophies of *outre mer*, in his dissatisfaction with the shallow dogmatism of the church and college of the pioneer. In all European philosophies since the time of Descartes the problem of knowledge had been central, the problem of relating the cognitive experience of the individual mind to the great structures of the physical universe which Newtonian science presented, and to the moral universe which western society in its states and churches predicated. Some of these structures were new and some were old, and at various points they clashed with each other. The scientific presentations demanded acceptance on the basis of objective evidence. When they clashed with inherited dogma the individual had to find within himself, if he attempted to think out his problem, the reason for acceptance or rejection. If the clash came between scientific doctrines evidence could be obtained from the findings. The scientist was not thrown back upon his own mind. But if the conflict arose between the dogmas in social institutions and scientific doctrine no such appeal could be made to accept findings. Western thought presupposed an ordered, intelligible, moral universe. Its ordered intelligible character, that is, its uniformity, enabled the mind to test its scientific findings, but its moral order presupposed a supreme end or purpose in which the purposes of voluntary individuals could appear as elements of an organized whole. However, no such ordered moral whole is given by which one may test his individual purpose. The same might be said of intelligible nature. No complete universe is given by which the scientist may test his hypothesis. But the scientist is quite willing to accept the experimental test of his hypothesis. His experience thus becomes a part of the objective world of science. For no modern scientist has skepticism been a practical problem. But the Western world has been obsessed with the conception of a given moral order with which the individual will must accord if the individual is to be moral. The scientist is not the less scientific because the hypothesis which he has brought to the experimental test is later proved to be incorrect. But the moral individual is good or bad as he has or has not conformed to the given moral order, and yet his judgment is fallible. Only Kant's rigorous but empty categorical imperative offers a seemingly logical escape from the dilemma. As it proved in the case of Kant and his idealistic successors, the established institutions of society offer the only palpable expressions of such a given moral order. Here skepticism is a practical problem. And it was out of attempted solution of the relation of the individual will and its purpose to a given all-inclusive aim of the absolute will that Royce's idealism arose.

Such skepticism has had its place in the American community, but it has belonged mainly to the adolescent over against the claims of the dogma of the church. It was not reflected in the general attitude of a community engaged in the reconstruction of its institutions. A striking difference between the spiritual lives of Europe and America, since the American revolution, is that a continuous process of revolution and reconstruction was going on in Europe while American institutions have been subject to no conscious reconstruction. The values embodied in the institutions of the European communities were felt to be profoundly threatened, or revolutionary parties sought to restate them in their own programs, or political and social reformers insisted that the changes they sought would not imperil them. In the background of all thought lay these values, and it is this sense of them in the face of the profound changes that were going on that gave to Europe in the nineteenth century its peculiar character. This same culture brought to American shores lacked this background of social reconstruction. It was foreign and yet it was our only culture. The dominance of middle-class ideals of contractual freedom, of political democracy, of freedom of the school from the church, these were commonplaces in American consciousness. The insurgence of these concepts and attitudes into an old feudally ordered society gave a rich setting for novelist, poet, and historian. The cultured American had to become a European to catch the flavor. He had to get another soul as does the man who has learned a new vernacular or who has traveled in foreign parts. Our own bitter struggle to abolish slavery that the country might remain a united community found little to illuminate and interpret it in this culture. The problem was not a European problem. Skepticism had a profound social import in Europe. The freethinker was not simply one who criticized theological dogma. He was a libertarian in a political sense and was thought to be endangering all institutions. It is only necessary to reflect upon socialism in Europe, and to think of the meaninglessness of it in the American community during the nineteenth century, to bring vividly to consciousness the profound difference between the European and the American minds. The results of this was that while there was a cultured group in the community, and while culture was sought vividly in institutions of learning, in lyceums and clubs, it did not reflect the political and economic activities which were fundamental in American life. We realize that Kant, Fichte, Schelling, and Hegel each stood for a phase of the reconstruction that was going on in the German community; and we realize that this romantic idealism was not so foreign to the English community that Green could not draw from this idealism a new and living sense of the individual in the community and the social reality that expressed itself in the individual. But one cannot dream of that philosophy interpreting the relation of the American individual to society. And yet the American philosopher had to acquire his detachment of thought, his sense of the philosophic problem, and his training in philosophic disciplines in these European philosophies. They were, of course, as much his as were the medieval doctrines of Thomas and Scotus, or the philosophies of Greece. But Royce did not present the problems of American consciousness in the terms of the older philosophies. They were recognizedly distant in history, but he did present the problem of the relation of the American individual to his universe, physical and moral, in terms of the absolute idealism that was at home in a German, almost a Prussian soil. It is only in a community in which personal subordination is sublimated into identification of the self with the larger social whole, where feudal social organization still persists, that romantic idealism can interpret the immediate problem of the individual to the world. It was the passionate struggle of Royce's great mind to fashion, in his philosophy of Loyalty, an expression of this idealism which would fit the problem of American thought. He was obliged to take it into the vernacular of the church, where alone skepticism had a meaning, to seek for reverberations from Calvinistic and Pauline conceptions. His individual was voluntaristic; the judgment was an expression of purpose. His individual is American in his attitude, but he calls upon this American to realize himself in an intellectual organization of conflicting ends that is already attained in the absolute self, and there is nothing in the relation of the American to his society that provides any mechanism that even by sublimation can accomplish such a realization. Not even in the Blessed Community, with Royce's social analysis of the self, does Royce lay hands upon an American social attitude that will express his undertaking. Causes, loyalty to which unites the man to the group, so far from fusing themselves with higher causes till loyalty reaches an ultimate loyalty to loyalty, remain particular and seek specific ends in practical conduct, not resolution in an attained harmony of disparate causes at infinity. Nor does Royce's stroke of genius—the infinite series involved in self-representation—reflect the self-consciousness of the American individual. The same remark may be made upon Royce's doctrine of interpretation. In each of these conceptions Royce points out that the individual reaches the self only by a process that implies still another self for its existence and thought. If the structure of reality that is organized about the self in the social process is already there, the concept affords a striking picture of its infinity. The logical implication, empty in itself, can interpret a structure if the structure is there and reveal its character. But the American even in his religious moments did not make use of his individualism—his self-consciousness—to discover the texture of reality. He did not think of himself as arising out of a society, so that by retiring into himself he could seize the nature of that society. On the contrary, the pioneer was creating communities and ceaselessly legislating changes within them. The communities came from him, not he from the community. And it followed that he did not hold the community in reverent respect.

We are not likely to exaggerate the critical importance of religion, as the carrier of the fundamental standards of social conduct, in the building up of the great American community; but it belonged to the character of the pioneer that his religious principles and doctrines like his political principles and doctrines were put into such shape that he could carry them about with him. They were part of the limited baggage with which he could trek into the unpeopled west. He was not interested in their origins or the implications of those origins, but in the practical uses to which they could be put. And no American, in his philosophical moments, regarding the sectarian meeting-houses of a western community would have felt itself at home in spiritual landscape of Royce's Blessed Community. Notwithstanding Royce's intense moral sense and his passionate love of the community from which he came and to which he continued to belong, his philosophy belonged, in spite of himself, to culture and to a culture which did not spring from the controlling habits and attitudes of American society. I can remember very vividly the fascination of the idealisms in Royce's luminous presentations. They were a part of that great world of *outre mer* and exalted my imagination as did its cathedrals, its castles, and all its romantic history. It was part of the escape from the crudity of American life, not an interpretation of it.

In the psychological philosophy of William James, on the other hand, we find purpose explaining and elucidating our cognition, rather than setting up a metaphysical problem which can only be solved by positing an infinite intellect. James's chapter on the concept is the source of his later pragmatism, and of the pregnant ideas which both Royce and Dewey confess that they owe to him. The passage from the percept to the concept is by way of attentive selection and the source of this attentive selection must be found in the act. Knowledge predicates conduct, and conduct sets the process within which it must be understood. Royce admits it, and considers the judgment an act, and then proceeds to draw metaphysical conclusions, if the universe is a moral universe. But for James the act is a living physiological affair, and must be placed in the struggle for existence, which Darwinian evolution had set up as the background of life. Knowledge is an expression of the intelligence by which animals meet the problems with which life surrounds them. The orientation of knowledge is changed. Its efficacy can be determined not by its agreement with a pre-existent reality but by its solution of the difficulty within which the act finds itself. Here we have the soil from which pragmatism sprang. Both Royce and James were influenced by the science of their period. Royce was affected by mathematical science at the point at which mathematics and logic coalesce, and he was a considerable figure in the development of symbolic logic. James's medical training brought him under the influence of the biological sciences. But back of this lay James's own individual problem—the skepticism of adolescence set in a long period of illness that sickened both body and mind. What could he believe that would give him the assurance with which to face life? He demanded the right to believe that he might live. There must be a meaning in life that transcended the mechanistic conception of it which the biological sciences presented. Renouvier fortified him in his refusal to surrender the will to mechanism. The mechanistic doctrine could not be proved, and his own will to believe pulled him out the pit.

James, though born in New York, was a New Englander. New England was the seat of the Puritan tradition and also the seat of culture, both that of the Old World and that which had continued to flourish in America. He had the keenest aesthetic response and had even tentatively addressed himself to the artist's life. Residence abroad had equipped him with European languages and made him at home in Europe, as he was at home in Boston and at Harvard, but his mental and moral citizenship was in America, as that of his brother Henry was not. In his own experience he was not aware of the break between the profound processes of American life and its culture. He was not of pioneer stock. He condemned the crudity, the political corruption, the materialism of American life, but he condemned it as an American. It was perhaps because the solution that he sought for his own problems did not take him to foreign systems, that it was out of his own physiology and psychology, that he felt his way to an intellectual and moral world within which he could live, that the cleavage between life and culture did not appear in his philosophy. His philosophy was a native American growth. The adolescent skepticism with which his mental struggles began was common to American youth who thought at all, and he found and fashioned within himself the weapons with which to defeat it. He lived and thought freely. If any man's culture has been a part of himself, this was true of James. He carried no burden of learning or critical apparatus, and he was instinctively responsive to what was native to other people. Like Goethe he was at home in any circle, but without Goethe's sophistication. And yet he remained a New Englander, as far as American life was concerned. The principle of his solution was found in the individual soul. His was a lofty individualism. He was ready to go to the help of the Lord against the mighty, and called on others to go with him, but it was as individuals they were to go, to bring more moral order into a pluralistic unfinished universe.

He heralded the scientific method in philosophy. The test of the hypothesis was in its working, and all ideas were hypotheses. Thinking was but a part of action, and action found its completion and its standards in consequences. He adopted Pierce's laboratory habit of mind. But what were the consequences? In the laboratory of the scientist the hypothesis—the idea—is fashioned in terms of anticipated consequences. The experiment must be adjusted to certain prevised events, if the experiment is to say anything. The control of conduct is as essential in the formation of ideas as in the culmination of the act which tests them. And here lies the whole case of pragmatism in its interpretation of knowledge, for if the idea comes into the act, without becoming a part of the apparatus for intelligent control in this situation, the consequences will not test the truth of the idea. They will reveal nothing but the attitude of the individual. Now from the early days in which James was fighting for a foothold of assurance in living, through the poignant thought brought to expression in the will to believe, in his profoundly sympathetic analysis of types of religious experience, and in the lectures on pragmatism, James faced ideas of freedom of the will, of God, and the moral order of the universe, which demanded acceptance of the individual, at the peril of the loss of the values they subtend. And James fought to make the attitude of the individual in these crises pragmatic evidence of the truth of these ideas. This led to the ambiguous term satisfaction as the test of truth. This predisposition inevitably blurred his analysis of knowledge in conduct and the nature of the idea. For all of his analysis of the self, James's individual remained a soul in his article on the moral philosopher, and even in his celebrated chapter on habit. It entered in advance of the situation it helped to determine. It carried standards and criteria within itself. It was still the American individual that had fashioned the ecclesiastical and political community within which it lived, though James was a New Englander and no pioneer and lived in a community old enough to have its own culture, though it was a culture that was in great measure sterile in the development of the larger American community. His individual had that in him which was not fashioned in the living process in which his intelligence arose.

John Dewey was also a New Englander like James, and like Royce he was intellectually bred in the idealisms of Kant, Fichte, Schelling, and Hegel, and can say today that

> If there be a synthesis in ultimate Being of the realities which can be cognitively substantiated and of meanings which should command our highest admiration and approval, then concrete phenomena,— ought to be capable of being exhibited as definite manifestations of the eternal union of the real-ideal,

though today this is for Dewey a condition contrary to fact. But while Royce went to Harvard, Dewey went to the University of Michigan. Both Dewey and Royce published psychologies, though Dewey's came earlier in the development of his thought, and constituted in its treatment of the will and the emotions an early step in the formulation of conduct as the field of experience. Like Royce, Dewey was profoundly influenced by James's psychology, though as I have already indicated it suggested to him a method of interpretation of knowledge rather than a metaphysical problem to be worked out in Hegelian fashion. As in the case of James, it was biological science with its dominant conception of evolution that offered him a process within which to analyze and place intelligence.

It would, however, be an error to ascribe to James's *Psychology* the starting-point of Dewey's independent thought. In his *Outline of Ethics*, 1891, in which are to be found the essential positions of his ethical doctrine, among his many acknowledgments to English idealistic and naturalistic writers, he makes no reference to James; and yet here we find him denouncing the "fallacy that moral action means something more than action itself." Here we find the "one moral reality—the full free play of human life," the "analysis of individuality into function including capacity and environment," and the "idea of desire as the ideal activity in contrast with actual possession." How far he had traveled from his earlier position appears from the following passage from an article printed in 1884. He there

> declares that God, as the perfect Personality or Will, is the only Reality, and the source of all activity. It is therefore the source of all activity of the individual personality. The Perfect Will is the motive, source, and realization of the life of the individual. He has renounced his own particular life as an unreality; he has asserted that the sole reality is the universal Will, and in that reality all his actions take place.[1]

In the *Outline of Ethics* we find the will, the idea, and the consequences all placed inside of the act, and the act itself placed only within the larger activity of the individual in society.

All reference of knowledge to a pre-existent ideal reality has disappeared. Knowledge refers to consequences imagined or experienced. Dewey passed out of his idealistic position by the way of the psychological analysis of the moral act. He occupied himself with the function of knowledge in doing. Instead of finding in the conflict of aims a problem, that knowledge can solve only in an absolute will, it becomes the immediate moral problem of the individual within the act. And his next step was by way of the school, in which he subjected his philos-

---

[1] I am indebted for this quotation to the thesis of Dr. Maurice Baum, entitled "A Comparative Study of the Philosophies of William James and John Dewey."

ophy to the more severe test of actual accomplishments in education. He accepted the headship of the Department of Philosophy at the University of Chicago upon the condition that it should include that of Education; and his earliest steps in the new field were in the establishment of the Experimental School, in which the education of the children was worked out upon the principle that knowing is a part of doing.

Now Pragmatism is recognized as a part of a current of thought which has had other expressions in other communities. Elsewhere in particular it has been allied with an anti-intellectualism, as for example in Bergson's philosophy. Two characteristics of this phase of modern thought may be noted, one the reference of thought to conduct, and the other the inclusion of intelligence within the sweep of biologic evolution. That these should lead to anti-intellectualism implies that intelligence and thought are not so native to human conduct and behavior even in their most elaborate social expressions, but that they deform experience. In other words, it is assumed that thought has the function not only of facilitating conduct but also of presenting reality as well. Even a theory of knowledge cannot serve two masters, and it was the task of freeing cognition from the shackles of a divided allegiance which Dewey accomplished in his *Essays in Experimental Logic*. Here Pierce's laboratory habit of mind follows through the whole process of knowing. In particular it is exhibited in elaboration of the problem from which it starts upon its experimental undertaking. In isolating the sense data, and the relations which the conflicts of experience have shaken out, in sharp logical distinction from the non-problematic world within which it arises, Dewey exempts the logical process that is seeking knowledge from any responsibility for the world that has set the problem. It frees having, enjoying, and suffering and the percept, as the statement of the object that is simply there, from a consciousness *of*, and the way is open for the more complete analysis of consciousness in *Experience and Nature*. The gist of it is that what had been already achieved for the moral act was now established for the act of knowing, and if cognition is not responsible for the world that sets the problem still less is it called upon to read back into a pre-existent reality its accomplishment in the solution of its problem, the "fallacy of conversion of eventual functions into antecedent existence." In *Experience and Nature* the parallelism between the analysis of the moral act and the cognitive act is completed. As it is shown in the former that it is in social participation that the peculiar character of the moral appears, so in the latter it is through the participation that is involved in communication, and hence in thought itself, that meaning arises. There is a grand simplicity in the advance from the *Syllabus* and *Outline of Ethics* in 1891 to *Experience and Nature* and *The Quest for Certainty* in 1929. As Whitehead has admonished us, "Seek for simplicity and then distrust it." It is a wise admonition, but before we address ourselves to the subtle problems and the difficult readjustments which any great reconstruction bring with it, we may stop to enjoy the sense of enormous relief with which one completes *The Quest for Certainty*. That baffled sense of the philosophic squirrel running a ceaseless dialectical round within his cage, that despairing sense of the philosophic Sisyphus vainly striving to roll the heavily weighted world of his reflexion up into a pre-existent reality—these drop away and the philosopher can face about toward the future and join in the scientist's adventure. Not the eagerness to grapple with a dialectical opponent, not the sense of escape into a city not built with hands, but the sense of freedom for action—it is a novel attitude in which to lay down a profound philosophic treatise.

It has been a term of opprobrium that has been cast upon Dewey's doctrine that it is the philosophy of American practicality. But now that the world has become somewhat more respectful of us and more curious about us it may not, perhaps, be opprobrious to recognize the relation of Dewey's habitat to his philosophic output. In the first place it was beyond the Alleghenies that he formulated his problem and worked out the essentials of his doctrine. Though Hegelianism flourished in a small and somewhat Teutonic group in St. Louis, which was not without its repercussions in America, as witness both Royce and Dewey, it was Royce who established the absolute idealisms in American thought by making them a part of culture. There was no sublimation of the individual in the structure of society in America which could make absolute idealism an outgrowth of American consciousness; but as a part of culture it took its place, and the center of gravity of this culture was in New England. I have indicated what seems to me the important characteristic of American life, the freedom, within certain rather rigid but very wide boundaries, to work out immediate politics and business with no reverential sense of a pre-existing social order within which they must take their place and whose values they must preserve. We refer to this as individualism, perhaps uncouth, but unafraid. In its finest form it was embodied in William James, for it was in him refined by a genuine native culture. Now there is only one way in which such an individualism can be brought under constructive criticism, and that is by bringing the individual to state his ends and purposes in terms of the social means he is using. You cannot get at him with an ethics from above, you *can* reach him by an ethics that is simply the development of the intelligence implicit in his act. I take it that it is such an implicit intelligence that has been responsible for the steady development and social integration that has taken place in the American community, with little leadership and almost entirely without ideas. It is hardly necessary to point out that John Dewey's philosophy, with its insistence upon the statement of the end in the terms of the means, is the developed method of that implicit intelligence in the mind of the American community. And for such an implicit intelligence there is no other test of moral and intellectual hypotheses except that they work. In the profoundest sense John Dewey is the philosopher of America.

13

The Working Hypothesis in
Social Reform*

HERE ARE SOME CONSEQUENCES that follow from the attempt to
establish the theory of social reform among the inductive sciences that need emphasis. That to which I wish to refer is the implication of the hypothesis.

Socialism, in one form or another, lies back of the thought directing
and inspiring reform. While socialistic utopias have been recognized
as impotent to lead to better conditions, and opportunists have succeeded to the programists, the assumption that it will be possible to
effect by constructive legislation radical changes that will lead to greater
social equality is still very widely present. The success of municipal
ownership, in means of transportation and various common necessities
within cities, has aroused the expectation that this success can be
achieved in other industries as fast as they are so organized as to become so-called natural monopolies. I think that a great deal of this
confidence is inspired by the socialistic schemes of an essentially *a priori*
character, rather than by a study of the conditions which these municipal
concerns represent. We fail often to notice that government as an institution has essentially changed its character in so far as it has assumed
these new functions. The government has become a business concern,
which enters into the business world on a basis that is determined by
the latter. It has assumed a certain amount of invested capital, where

* As originally published in the *American Journal of Sociology*, V (1899),
367–71.

business risk has ceased, in the interests of its members, and has undertaken to carry on an enterprise that has already been worked out as regards its methods and technique. In a word, the municipality has become a business body operating for the benefit of those that make it up, and is therefore not different in principle from any stock company. The number of enterprises that such a body could undertake as a commercial body are, so far, necessarily small, and we have no reason to assume that in the end anything but business conditions will determine what the municipality may successfully manage. There is no reason why the German government, as a social individual, should not buy up and manage such a business as the railroad; only so far as the business itself is concerned it must conduct it upon the principles which control the industrial world as a whole. It may introduce such reforms into it as are demanded by the public sentiment that finds expression in legislation, sooner than they will be introduced into other concerns. But it becomes at once in tendency as conservative as other great concerns, and must adapt itself to the demands of the business world of which it is a part. The government has then separate functions. On the one side, it formulates and brings to a focus public sentiment in so-called legislation, and conducts a police activity, national and international, over against classes of society and human impulses which are as yet not so socially organized as are the bulk of its members with their dominant impulses. On the other side, being an institution which is as definitely independent as other corporations within the community, it may undertake a very limited number of industrial and commercial concerns, which business evolution has carried to such a point of perfection that they lie safely within its domain.

While we recognize this possibility, we must, on the other side, recognize with equal distinctness that the functions of government, as an institution, are merging with equal rapidity into the industrial world which it is supposed to control. The whole work of legislation is not only dependent upon public sentiment, at least in democratic countries, but it is finding constantly fuller expression in other channels of publicity. The newspaper, in its various forms of journal and magazine, is effecting changes that are assumed to be those which follow governmental action. If only it becomes possible to focus public sentiment upon an issue in the delicate organism of the modern civilized community, it is as effective as if the mandate came from legislative halls, and frequently more so. This is true, not simply in the public reaction upon the justice of movements like those of great strikes and lockouts, but even in the interpretation of the methods of industrial and commercial activity. What the court does in reinterpreting laws is being done in increasing extent by simply closer organization of the business world—an organization that depends most immediately upon growing publicity. The study of the criminal and defective classes, as an expression of the conditions of the social body in which they are found, and their treatment from this new standpoint, as well as the movement toward arbitration for the solution of international differences, all point to the passing of functions which are supposed to inhere in the government into activities that belong to the community simply through its organization apart from government as a separate institution. On the other hand, certainly one of the most important so-called governmental functions, that is characteristic of the time, is the committee work, which is but a part of the general process of gaining publicity as regards what is going on in the country and the world. This is often done, not by a legislative commission, but by the university as well as the newspaper. In attempting to forecast what is to be the result of the movement of municipal ownership, we have to consider, therefore, not only the development of the municipal corporation and the industry that it conducts, but also that of a government that is changing fully as rapidly as the industrial and commercial world.

I have adduced this as an illustration of the attitude which social reformers must assume toward their problems. It is impossible to so forecast any future condition that depends upon the evolution of society as to be able to govern our conduct by such a forecast. It is always the unexpected that happens, for we have to recognize, not only the immediate change that is to take place, but also the reaction back upon this of the whole world within which the change takes place, and no human foresight is equal to this. In the social world we must recognize the working hypothesis as the form into which all theories must be cast as completely as in the natural sciences. The highest criterion that we can present is that the hypothesis shall *work* in the complex of forces into which we introduce it. We can never set up a detailed statement of the conditions that are to be ultimately attained. What we have is a method and a control in application, not an ideal to work toward. As has been stated, this is the attitude of the scientist in the laboratory, whether his work remains purely scientific or is applied immediately to conduct. His foresight does not go beyond the testing of his hypothesis. Given its success, he may restate his work from this standpoint and get the basis for further investigation that again always takes the form of a problem. The solution of this problem is found over again in the possibility of fitting his hypothetical proposition into the whole within which it arises. And he must recognize that this statement is only a working hypothesis at the best, *i.e.*, he knows that further investigation will show that the former statement of his world is only provisionally true, and must be false from the standpoint of a larger knowledge, as every partial truth is necessarily taken over against the fuller knowledge which he will gain later. Even the axioms of Euclid are not true now in the sense of Euclid. In a word, our confidence in the results of science and the general application of intelligence to the control of the physical world is based, not upon a knowledge of the whole universe as it is, but upon a faith in its general rational character, that is perhaps best stated in the success of working hypotheses.

In social reform, or the application of intelligence to the control of social conditions, we must make a like assumption and this assumption takes the form of belief in the essentially social character of human impulse and endeavor. We cannot make persons social by legislative enactment, but we can allow the essentially social nature of their actions to come to expression under conditions which favor this. What the form of this social organization will be depends upon conditions that lie necessarily beyond our ken. We assume that human society is governed by laws that involve its solidarity, and we seek to find these out that they may be used. In the same way the natural scientist assumes that the world is as a whole governed by laws that involve the interaction of all its forces, and that he must find these laws out, and use them for the further organization of his world, so far as he is a part of it.

There is here, however, a distinction that is of considerable importance. In the physical world we regard ourselves as standing in some degree outside the forces at work, and thus avoid the difficulty of harmonizing the feeling of human initiative with the recognition of series which are necessarily determined. In society we are the forces that are being investigated, and if we advance beyond the mere description of the phenomena of the social world to the attempt at reform, we seem to involve the possibility of changing what at the same time we assume to be necessarily fixed. The question, stated more generally, is: What is the function of reflective consciousness in its attempt to direct conduct? The common answer is that we carry in thought the world as it should be, and fashion our conduct to bring this about. As we have already seen, if this implies a "vision given in the mount" which represents in detail what is to be, we are utterly incapable of conceiving it. And every attempt to direct conduct by a fixed idea of the world of the future must be, not only a failure, but also pernicious. A conception of a different world comes to us always as the result of some specific problem which involves readjustment of the world as it is, not to meet a detailed ideal of a perfect universe, but to obviate the present difficulty; and the test of the effort lies in the possibility of this readjustment fitting into the world as it is. Reflective consciousness does not then carry us on to the world that is to be, but puts our own thought and endeavor into the very process of evolution, and evolution within consciousness that has become reflective has the advantage over other evolution in that the form does not tend to perpetuate himself as he is, but identifies himself with the process of development. Our reflective consciousness as applied to conduct is, therefore, an identification of our effort with the problem that presents itself, and the developmental process by which it is overcome, and reaches its highest expression in the scientific statement of the problem, and the recognition and use of scientific method and control.

14

The Psychology of Punitive Justice*

THE STUDY OF INSTINCTS on the one side and of the motor character of human conduct upon the other has given us a different picture of human nature from that which a dogmatic doctrine of the soul and an intellectualistic psychology presented to an earlier generation.

The instincts even in the lower animal forms have lost their rigidity. They are found to be subject to modification by experience, and the nature of the animal is found to be not a bundle of instincts but an organization within which these congenital habits function to bring about complex acts—acts which are in many cases the result of instincts which have modified each other. Thus new activities arise which are not the simple expression of bare instincts. A striking illustration of this is found in play, especially among young animal forms, in which the hostile instinct is modified and held in check by the others that dominate the social life of the animals. Again the care which the parent form gives to the infant animal admits of hostile features which, however, do not attain the full expression of attack and destruction usually involved in the instinct from which they arise. Nor is this merging and interaction of such divergent instinctive acts a process of alternate dominance of now one and now another instinct. Play and parental care may be and generally are of a piece, in which the inhibition of one tendency by the others has entered into the structure of the animal's nature and seemingly even of its congenital nervous orga-

* As originally published in the *American Journal of Sociology*, XXIII (1917–1918), 577–602.

nization. Another illustration of such a merging of divergent instincts is found in the elaborate wooing of the female among the birds.

Back of all this type of organization of instinctive conduct lies the social life within which there must be co-operation of the different individuals, and therefore a continual adjustment of the responses to the changing attitudes of the animals that participate in the corporate acts. It is this body of organized instinctive reactions to one another which makes up the social nature of these forms, and it is from a social nature of this kind exhibited in the conduct of lower forms that our human nature is evolved. An elaborate analysis of this is still in the making, but certain great features in it stand out with sufficient clearness to warrant comment. We find two opposing groups of instincts, those which we have named hostile and those which may be termed friendly, the latter being largely combinations of the parental and sexual instincts. The import of a herding instinct lying back of them all is still very uncertain if not dubious. What we do find is that individuals adjust themselves to each other in common social processes, but come into conflict with each other frequently in the process, that the expression of this individual hostility within the whole social act is primarily that of the destructive hostile type modified and molded by the organized social reaction, that where this modification and control breaks down, as, e.g., in the rivalry of males in the herd or pack, the hostile instinct may assert itself in its native ruthlessness.

If we turn to the human nature that has developed out of the social nature of lower animals, we find in addition to the organization of social conduct that I have indicated a vast elaboration of the process of adjustment of individuals to each other. This elaboration of gesture, to use Wundt's generalized term, reaches its most developed expression in language. Now language was first the attitude, glance of the eye, movement of the body and its parts indicating the oncoming social act to which the other individuals must adjust their conduct. It becomes language in the narrower sense when it is a common speech of whatever form; that is when through his gesture the individual addresses *himself* as well as the others who are involved in the act. His speech is their speech. He can address himself in their gestures and thus present to himself the whole social situation within which he is involved, so that not only is conduct social but consciousness becomes social as well.

It is out of this conduct and this consciousness that human society grows. What gives it its human character is that the individual through language addresses himself in the rôle of the others in the group and thus becomes aware of them in his own conduct. But while this phase of evolution is perhaps the most critical in the development of man, it is after all only an elaboration of the social conduct of lower forms. Self-conscious conduct is only an exponent which raises the possible complications of group activity to a higher degree. It does not change the character of the social nature that is elaborated and complicated, nor does it change the principles of its organization. Human nature still remains an organization of instincts which have mutually affected each other. Out of such fundamental instincts as those of sex, parenthood, and hostility has arisen an organized type of social conduct, the conduct of the individual within the group. The attack upon the other individuals of the group has been modified and softened so that the individual asserts himself as over against the others in play, in courting, in care of the young, in certain common attitudes of attack and defense, without the attempted destruction of the individuals attacked. If we use the common terminology we shall account for these modifications by the process of trial and error within the evolution out of which has arisen the social form. Out of the hostile instinct has arisen conduct modified by the social instincts that has served to delimit the conduct springing from sex, parenthood, and mutual defense and attack. It has been the function of the hostile instinct to provide the reaction by which the individual asserts himself within a social process, thus modifying that process while the hostile conduct is itself modified *pro tanto*. The result is the appearance of new individuals, certain types of sex mates, playmates, parent and child forms, mates in fight and mates in defense. While this assertion of the individual within the social process delimits and checks the social act at various points, it leads to a modified social response with a new field of operation which did not exist for the unmodified instincts. The source of these higher complexes of social conduct appears suddenly when through a breakdown of the organization of the social act there is enacted a crime of passion, the direct outcome of self-assertion within sex, family, or other group responses. Unmodified self-assertion under these conditions means the destruction of the individual attacked.

When now, through the exponent of self-consciousness, the complexities of social conduct are raised to the nth power, when the individual addresses himself as well as the others by his gestures, when in the rôle of another he can respond to his own stimulus, all the range of possible activities is brought within the field of social conduct. He finds himself within groups of varied sorts. The size of the group to which he can belong is limited only by his ability to co-operate with its members. Now the common control over the food process lifts these instincts out of the level of the mechanical response to biologically determined stimuli and brings them within the sweep of self-conscious direction inside of the larger group activity. And these varied groupings multiply the occasions of individual oppositions. Here again the instinct of hostility becomes the method of self-assertion, but while the oppositions are self-conscious the process of readjustment and the molding of the hostile attitudes by the larger social process remains in principle the same, though the long road of trial and error may be at times abandoned for the short cuts which the symbolism of language provides.

On the other hand the consciousness of self through consciousness of others is responsible for a more profound sense of hostility—that of the members of the groups to those opposed to it, or even to those merely outside it. And this hostility has the backing of the whole inner organization of the group. It provides the most favorable condition for the sense of group solidarity because in the common attack upon the common enemy the individual differences are obliterated. But in the development of these group hostilities we find the same self-assertion with the attempted elimination of the enemy giving way before the larger social whole within which the conflicting groups find themselves. The hostile self-assertion passes over into functional activities in the new type of conduct as it has taken place in play even among lower animal forms. The individual becomes aware of himself, not through the conquest of the other, but through the distinction of function. It is not so much that the actual hostile reactions are themselves transformed as that the individual who is conscious of himself as over against the enemy finds other opportunities for conduct which remove the immediate stimuli for destroying the enemy. Thus the conqueror who realized himself in his power of life or death over the captive found in the industrial value of the slave a new attitude which removed the sense of hostility and opened the door to that economic development which finally placed the two upon the same ground of common citizenship.

It is in so far as the opposition reveals a larger underlying relationship within which the hostile individuals arouse non-hostile reactions that the hostile reactions themselves become modified into a type of self-assertion which is balanced against the self-assertion of those who had been enemies, until finally these oppositions become the compensating activities of different individuals in a new social conduct. In other words the hostile instinct has the function of the *assertion* of the social self when this self comes into existence in the evolution of human behavior. The man who has achieved an economic, a legal, or any type of social triumph does not feel the impulse to physically annihilate his opponent, and ultimately the mere sense of the security of his social position may rob the stimulus to attack of all of its power.

The moral of this is, and one is certainly justified in emphasizing

133

it at this time of a profound democratic movement in the midst of a world-war, that advance takes place in bringing to consciousness the larger social whole within which hostile attitudes pass over into self-assertions that are functional instead of destructive.

The following pages discuss the hostile attitude as it appears especially in punitive justice.

In the criminal court it is the purpose of the proceeding to prove that the defendant did or did not commit a certain act, that in case the defendant did commit the act this act falls under such and such a category of crime or misdemeanor as defined by the statute, and that, as a consequence, he is subject to such and such punishment. It is the assumption of this procedure that conviction and punishment are the accomplishment of justice and also that it is for the good of society, that is, that it is both just and expedient, though it is not assumed that in any particular case the meting out to a criminal of the legal recompense of his crime will accomplish an immediate social good which will outweigh the immediate social evil that may result to him, his family, and society itself from his conviction and imprisonment. Galsworthy's play *Justice* turns upon the wide discrepancy between legal justice and social good in a particular case. On the other side lies the belief that without this legal justice with all its miscarriages and disintegrating results society itself would be impossible. In the back of the public mind lie both these standards of criminal justice, that of retribution and that of prevention. It is just that a criminal should suffer in proportion to the evil that he has done. On the other hand it is just that the criminal should suffer so much and in such a manner that his penalty will serve to deter him and others from committing the like offense in the future. There has been a manifest shift in the emphasis upon these two standards. During the Middle Ages, when courts of justice were the antechambers to chambers of torture, the emphasis lay upon the nice proportioning of the suffering to the offense. In the grand epic manner Dante projected this torture chamber, as the accomplishment of justice, against the sphere of the heavens, and produced those magnificent distortions and magnifications of human primitive vengeance that the medieval heart and imagination accepted as divine.

There existed, however, even then no commensurability between retributory sufferings and the evil for which the criminal was held responsible. In the last analysis he suffered until satisfaction had been given to the outraged sentiments of the injured person, or of his kith and kin, or of the community, or of an angry God. To satisfy the latter an eternity might be too short, while a merciful death ultimately carried away from the most exacting community the victim who was paying for his sin in the coin of his own agony. Commensurability does not exist between sin and suffering but does exist roughly between the sin and the amount and kind of suffering that will satisfy those who feel themselves aggrieved and yet it has become the judgment of our common moral consciousness that satisfaction in the suffering of the criminal has no legitimate place in assessing his punishment. Even in its sublimated form, as a part of righteous indignation, we recognize its legitimacy only in resenting and condemning injury, not in rendering justice for the evil done. It was therefore natural that in measuring the punishment the emphasis should shift from retribution to prevention, for there is a rough quantitative relation between the severity of the penalty and the fear which it inspires. This shift to the standard of expediency in determining the severity of the penalty does not mean that retribution is no longer the justification for punishment either in the popular mind or in legal theory, for however expedient it may be to visit crimes with condign punishments in the interest of the welfare of society, the justification for inflicting the suffering at all is found in the assumption that the criminal owes retributive suffering to the community; a debt which the community may collect in the form and amount which is most expedient to itself.

This curious combination of the concepts of retributive suffering which is the justification for punishment but may not be the standard for the amount and degree of the punishment, and of a social expediency which may not be the justification for the punishment itself but is the standard of the amount and kind of punishment inflicted, is evidently not the whole story. If retribution were the only justification for punishment it is hard to believe that punishment would not itself have disappeared when society came to recognize that a possible theory of punishment could not be worked out or maintained on the basis of retribution; especially when we recognize that a system of punishments assessed with reference to their deterrent powers not only works very inadequately in repressing crime but also preserves a criminal class. This other part of the story, which neither retribution nor social expediency tells, reveals itself in the assumed solemnity of criminal court procedure, in the majesty of the law, in the supposedly impartial and impersonal character of justice. These characters are not involved in the concept of retribution nor in that of deterrence. Lynch law is the very essence of retribution and is inspired with the grim assurance that such summary justice must strike terror into the heart of the prospective criminal, and lynch law lacks solemnity, and majesty, and is anything but impersonal or impartial. These characters inhere, not in the primitive impulses out of which punitive justice has arisen nor in the cautious prudence with which society devises protection for its goods, but in the judicial institution which theoretically acts on rule and not upon impulse and whose justice is to be done though the heavens fall. What, then, are these values evidenced in and maintained by the laws of punitive justice? The most patent value is the theoretically impartial enforcement of the common will. It is a procedure which undertakes to recognize and protect the individual in the interest of the common good and by the common will. In his acceptance of the law and dependence upon it the individual is at one with the community, while this very attitude carries with it the recognition of his responsibility to obey and support the law in its enforcement. So conceived the common law is an affirmation of citizenship. It is, however, a grave mistake to assume that the law itself and men's attitudes toward it can exist *in abstracto*. It is a grave mistake, for too often the respect for law as law is what we demand of members of the community, while we are able to regard with comparative indifference defects both in the concrete laws and in their administration. It is not only a mistake, it is also a fundamental error, for all emotional attitudes—and even respect for law and a sense of responsibility are emotional attitudes—arise in response to concrete impulses. We do not respect law in the abstract but the values which the laws of the community conserve. We have no sense of responsibility as such but an emotional recognition of duties which our position in the community entails. Nor are these impulses and emotional reactions less concrete because they are so organized into complex habits that some slight but appropriate stimulus sets a whole complex of impulses into operation. A man who defends an apparently unimportant right on principle is defending the whole body of analogous rights which a vast complex of social habits tends to preserve. His emotional attitude, which is seemingly out of proportion to the immediate issue, answers to all of those social goods toward which the different impulses in the organized body of habits are directed. Nor may we assume that because our emotions answer to concrete impulses they are therefore necessarily egoistic or self-regarding. No small portion of the impulses which make up the human individual are immediately concerned with the good of others. The escape from selfishness is not by the Kantian road of an emotional response to the abtract universal, but by the recognition of the genuinely social character of human nature. An important instance of this illusory respect for abstract law appears in our attitude of dependence upon the law and its enforcement for the defense of our goods and those of others with whom we identify our interests.

A threatened attack upon these values places us in an attitude of defense, and as this defense is largely intrusted to the operation of the laws of the land we gain a respect for the laws which is in proportion to the goods which they defend. There is, however, another attitude more easily aroused under these conditions which is, I think, largely responsible for our respect for law as law. I refer to the attitude of hostility to the lawbreaker as an enemy to the society to which we belong. In this attitude we are defending the social structure against an enemy with all the animus which the threat to our own interests calls out. It is not the detailed operation of the law in defining the invasion of rights and their proper preservation that is the center of our interest but the capture and punishment of the personal enemy, who is also the public enemy. The law is the bulwark of our interests, and the hostile procedure against the enemy arouses a feeling of attachment due to the means put at our disposal for satisfying the hostile impulse. The law has become the weapon for overwhelming the thief of our purses, our good names, or even of our lives. We feel toward it as we feel toward the police officer who rescues us from a murderous assault. The respect for the law is the obverse side of our hatred for the criminal aggressor. Furthermore the court procedure, after the man accused of the crime is put under arrest and has been brought to trial, emphasizes this emotional attitude. The state's attorney seeks a conviction. The accused must defend himself against this attack. The aggrieved person and the community find in this officer of the government their champion. A legal battle takes the place of the former physical struggle which led up to the arrest. The emotions called out are the emotions of battle. The impartiality of the court who sits as the adjudicator is the impartiality of the umpire between the contending parties. The assumption that contending parties will each do his utmost to win, places upon each, even upon the state's attorney, the obligation to get a verdict for his own side rather than to bring about a result which will be for the best interests of all concerned. The doctrine that the strict enforcement of the law in this fashion is for the best interest of all concerned has no bearing upon the point which I am trying to emphasize. This point is that the emotional attitude of the injured individual and of the other party to the proceedings—the community—toward the law is that engendered by a hostile enterprise in which the law has become the ponderous weapon of defense and attack.[1]

---

[1] I am referring here to criminal law and its enforcement, not only because respect for the law and the majesty of the law have reference almost entirely to criminal justice, but also because a very large part, perhaps the largest part, of civil law proceedings are undertaken and carried out with the intent of defining and readjusting social situations without the hostile attitudes which characterize the criminal procedure. The parties to the civil proceedings belong to the same group and continue to belong to this group, whatever decision is rendered. No stigma attaches to the one who loses. Our emotional attitude toward this body of law is that of interest, of condemnation and approval as it fails or succeeds in its social function. It is not an institution that must be respected even in its disastrous failures. On the contrary it must be changed. It is hedged about in our feelings by no majesty. It is efficient or inefficient and as such awakens satisfaction or dissatisfaction and an interest in its reform which is in proportion to the social values concerned.

There is another emotional content involved in this attitude of respect for law as law, which is perhaps of like importance with the other. I refer to that accompanying stigma placed upon the criminal. The revulsions against criminality reveal themselves in a sense of solidarity with the group, a sense of being a citizen which on the one hand excludes those who have transgressed the laws of the group and on the other inhibits tendencies to criminal acts in the citizen himself. It is this emotional reaction against conduct which excludes from society that gives to the moral taboos of the group such impressiveness. The majesty of the law is that of the angel with the fiery sword at the gate who can cut one off from the world to which he belongs. The majesty of the law is the dominance of the group over the individual, and the paraphernalia of criminal law serves not only to exile the rebellious individual from the group, but also to awaken in law-abiding members of society the inhibitions which make rebellion impossible to them. The formulation of these inhibitions is the basis of criminal law. The emotional content that accompanies them is a large part of the respect for law as law. In both these elements of our respect for law as law, in the respect for the common instrument of defense from and attack upon the enemy of ourselves and of society, and in the respect for that body of formulated custom which at once identifies us with the whole community and excludes those who break its commandments, we recognize concrete impulses—those of attack upon the enemy of ourselves and at the same time of the community, and those of inhibition and restraint through which we feel the common will, in the identity of prohibition and of exclusion. They are concrete impulses which at once identify us with the predominant whole and at the same time place us on the level of every other member of the group, and thus set up that theoretical impartiality and evenhandedness of punitive justice which calls out in no small degree our sense of loyalty and respect. And it is out of the universality that belongs to the sense of common action springing out of these impulses that the institutions of law and of regulative and repressive justice arise. While these impulses are concrete in respect of their immediate object, i.e., the criminal, the values which this hostile attitude toward the criminal protects either in society or in ourselves are negatively and abstractly conceived. Instinctively we estimate the worth of the goods protected by the procedure against the criminal and in terms of this hostile procedure. These goods are not simply the physical articles but include the more precious values of self-respect, in not allowing one's self to be overridden, in downing the enemy of the group, in affirming the maxims of the group and its institutions against invasions. Now in all of this we have our backs toward that which we protect and our faces toward the actual or potential enemy. These goods are regarded as valuable because we are willing to fight and even die for them in certain exigencies, but their intrinsic value is neither affirmed nor considered in the legal proceeding. The values thus obtained are not their values in use but sacrifice values. To many a man his country has become infinitely valuable because he finds himself willing to fight and die for it when the common impulse of attack upon the common enemy has been aroused, and yet he may have been, in his daily life, a traitor to the social values he is dying to protect because there was no emotional situation within which these values appeared in his consciousness. It is difficult to bring into commensurable relationship to each other a man's willingness to cheat his country out of its legitimate taxes and his willingness to fight and die for the same country. The reactions spring from different sets of impulses and lead to evaluations which seem to have nothing in common with each other. The type of valuation of social goods that arises out of the hostile attitude toward the criminal is negative, because it does not present the positive social function of the goods that the hostile procedure protects. From the standpoint of protection one thing behind the wall has the same import as anything else that lies behind the same defense. The respect for law as law thus is found to be a respect for a social organization of defense against the enemy of the group and a legal and judicial procedure that are oriented with reference to the criminal. The attempt to utilize these social attitudes and procedures to remove the causes of crime, to assess the kind and amount of punishment which the criminal should suffer in the interest of society, or to reinstate the criminal as a law-abiding citizen has failed utterly. For while the institutions which inspire our respect are concrete institutions with a definite function, they are responsible for a quite abstract and inadequate evaluation of society and its goods. These legal and political institutions organized with reference to the enemy or at least the outsider give a statement of social goods which is based upon defense and not upon function. The aim of the criminal proceeding is to determine whether the accused is innocent, i.e., still belongs to the group or whether he is guilty, i.e., is put under the ban which criminal punishment carries with it. The technical statement of this is found in the loss of the privileges of a citizen, in sentences of any severity, but the more serious ban is found in the fixed attitude of hostility on the part of the community toward a jailbird. One effect of this is to define the goods and privileges of the members of the community as theirs in virtue of their being law-abiding, and their responsibilities as exhausted by the statutes which determine the nature of criminal conduct. This effect is not due alone to the logical tendency to maintain the same definition of the institution of property over against the conduct of the thief and that of the law-abiding citizen. It is due in far greater degree to the feeling that we all stand together in the protection of property. In the positive definition of property, that is in terms of its social uses and functions, we are met by wide diversity of opinion, especially where the theoretically wide freedom of control over private property, asserted over against the thief, is restrained in the interest of problematic public goods. Out of this attitude toward the goods which the criminal law protects arises that fundamental difficulty in social reform which is due, not to mere difference in opinion nor to conscious selfishness, but to the fact that what we term opinions are profound social attitudes which, once assumed, fuse all conflicting tendencies over against the enemy of the people. The respect for law as law in its positive use in defense of social goods becomes unwittingly a respect for the conceptions of these goods which the attitude of defense has fashioned. Property becomes sacred not because of its social uses but because all the community is as one in its defense, and this conception of property, taken over into the social struggle to make property serve its functions in the community, becomes the bulwark of these in possession, *beati possidentes*.

Beside property other institutions have arisen, that of the person with its rights, that of the family with its rights, and that of the government with its rights. Wherever rights exist, invasion of those rights may be punished, and a definition of these institutions is formulated in protecting the right against trespass. The definition is again the voice of the community as a whole proclaiming and penalizing the one whose conduct has placed him under the ban. There is the same unfortunate circumstance that the law speaking against the criminal gives the sanction of the sovereign authority of the community to the negative definition of the right. It is defined in terms of its contemplated invasion. The individual who is defending his own rights against the trespasser is led to state even his family and more general social interests in abstract individualistic terms. Abstract individualism and a negative conception of liberty in terms of the freedom from restraints become the working ideas in the community. They have the prestige of battle cries in the fight for freedom against privilege. They are still the countersigns of the descendants of those who cast off the bonds of political and social restraint in their defense and assertion of the rights their forefathers won. Wherever criminal justice, the modern elaborate development of the taboo, the ban, and their consequences in a primitive society, organizes and formulates public sentiment in defense of social goods and institutions against actual or prospective enemies, there we find that the definition of the enemies, in other words the criminals, carries with it the definition of the goods and institutions. It is the revenge of the criminal upon the society which crushes him. The concentration of public sentiment upon the criminal which mobilizes the institution of justice, paralyzes the undertaking to conceive our common goods in terms of their uses. The majesty of the law is that of the sword drawn against a common enemy. The even-handedness of justice is that of universal conscription against a common enemy, and that of the abstract definition of rights which places the ban upon anyone who falls outside of its rigid terms.

Thus we see society almost helpless in the grip of the hostile attitude it has taken toward those who break its laws and contravene its institutions. Hostility toward the lawbreaker inevitably brings with it the attitudes of retribution, repression, and exclusion. These provide no principles for the eradication of crime, for returning the delinquent to normal social relations, nor for stating the transgressed rights and institutions in terms of their positive social functions.

On the other side of the ledger stands the fact that the attitude of hostility toward the lawbreaker has the unique advantage of uniting all members of the community in the emotional solidarity of aggression. While the most admirable of humanitarian efforts are sure to run counter to the individual interests of very many in the community, or fail to touch the interest and imagination of the multitude and to leave the community divided or indifferent, the cry of thief or murder is attuned to profound complexes, lying below the surface of competing individual effort, and citizens who have separated by divergent interests stand together against the common enemy. Furthermore, the attitude reveals common, universal values which underlie like a bedrock the divergent structures of individual ends that are mutually closed and hostile to each other. Seemingly without the criminal the cohesiveness of society would disappear and the universal goods of the community would crumble into mutually repellent individual particles. The criminal does not seriously endanger the structure of society by his destructive activities, and on the other hand he is responsibile for a sense of solidarity, aroused among those whose attention would be otherwise centered upon interests quite divergent from those of each other. Thus courts of criminal justice may be essential to the preservation of society even when we take account of the impotence of the criminal over against society, and the clumsy failure of criminal law in the repression and suppression of crime. I am willing to admit that this statement is distorted, not however in its analysis of the efficacy of the procedure against the criminal, but in its failure to recognize the growing consciousness of the many common interests which is slowly changing our institutional conception of society, and its consequent exaggerated estimate upon the import of the criminal. But it is important that we should realize what the implications of this attitude of hostility are within our society. We should especially recognize the inevitable limitations which the attitude carries with it. Social organization which arises out of hostility at once emphasizes the character which is the basis of the opposition and tends to suppress all other characters in the members of the group. The cry of "stop thief" unites us all as property owners against the robber. We all stand shoulder to shoulder as Americans against a possible invader. Just in proportion as we organize by hostility do we suppress individuality. In a political compaign that is fought on party lines the members of the party surrender themselves to the party. They become simply members of the party whose conscious aim is to defeat the rival organization. For this purpose the party member becomes merely a Republican or a Democrat. The party symbol expresses everything. Where simple social aggression or defense with the purpose of eliminating or encysting an enemy is the purpose of the community, organization through the common attitude of hostility is normal and effective. But as long as the social organization is dominated by the attitude of hostility the individuals or groups who are the objectives of this organization will remain enemies. It is quite impossible psychologically to hate the sin and love the sinner. We are very much given to cheating ourselves in this regard. We assume that we can detect, pursue, indict, prosecute, and punish the criminal and still retain toward him the attitude of reinstating him in the community as soon as he indicates a change in social attitude himself, that we can at the same time watch for the definite transgression of the statute to catch and overwhelm the offender, and comprehend the situation out of which the offense grows. But the two attitudes, that of control of crime by the hostile procedure of the law and that of control through comprehension of social and psychological conditions, cannot be combined. To understand is to forgive and the social procedure seems to deny the very responsibility which the law affirms, and on the other hand the pursuit by criminal justice inevitably awakens the hostile attitude in the offender and renders the attitude of mutual comprehension practically impossible. The social worker in the court is the sentimentalist, and the legalist in the social settlement in spite of his learned doctrine is the ignoramus.

While then the attitude of hostility, either against the transgressor of the laws or against the external enemy, gives to the group a sense of solidarity which most readily arouses like a burning flame and which consumes the differences of individual interests, the price paid for this solidarity of feeling is great and at times disastrous. Though human attitudes are far older than any human institutions and seem to retain identities of structure that make us at home in the heart of every man whose story has come down to us from the written and unwritten past, yet these attitudes take on new forms as they gather new social contents. The hostilities which flamed up between man and man, between family and family, and fixed the forms of old societies have changed as men came to realize the common whole within which these deadly struggles were fought out. Through rivalries, competitions, and co-operations men achieved the conception of a social state in which they asserted themselves while they at the same time affirmed the status of the others, on the basis not only of common rights and privileges but also on the basis of differences of interest and function, in an organization of more varied individuals. In the modern economic world a man is able to assert himself much more effectively against others through his acknowledgment of common property rights underlying their whole economic activity; while he demands acknowledgment for his individual competitive effort by recognizing and utilizing the varied activities and economic functions of others in the whole business complex.

This evolution reaches a still richer content when the self-assertion appears in the consciousness of social contribution that obtains the esteem of the others whose activities it complements and renders possible. In the world of scientific research rivalries do not preclude the warm recognition of the service which the work of one scientist renders to the whole co-operative undertaking of the *monde savante*. It is evident that such a social organization is not obtainable at will, but is dependent upon the slow growth of very varied and intricate social mechanisms. While no clearly definable set of conditions can be presented as responsible for this growth, it will I think be admitted that a very necessary condition, perhaps the most important one, is that of overcoming the temporal and spatial separations of men so that they are brought into closer interrelation with each other. Means of intercommunications have been the great civilizing agents. The multiple social stimulation of an indefinite number of varied contacts of a vast number of individuals with each other is the fertile field out of which spring social organizations, for these make possible the larger social life that can absorb the hostilities of different groups. When this condition has been supplied there seems to be an inherent tendency in social groups to advance from the hostile attitudes of individuals and groups toward each other through rivalries, competitions, and co-operations toward a functional self-assertion which recognize and utilizes other selves and groups of selves in the activities in which social human nature expresses itself. And yet the attitude of hostility of a community toward those who have transgressed its laws or customs, i.e., its criminals, and toward the outer enemies has remained as a great solidifying power. The passionate appreciation of our religious, political, property, and family institutions has arisen in the attack upon those who individually or collectively have assailed or violated them, and hostility toward the actual or prospective enemies of our country has been the never-failing source of patriotism.

If then we undertake to deal with the causes of crime in a fundamental way, and as dispassionately as we are dealing with the causes of disease, and if we wish to substitute negotiation and international adjudication for war in settling dispute between nations, it is of some importance to consider what sort of emotional solidarity we can secure to replace that which the traditional procedures have supplied. It is in the juvenile court that we meet the undertaking to reach and understand the causes of social and individual breakdown, to mend if possible the defective situation and reinstate the individual at fault. This is not attended with any weakening of the sense of the values that are at stake, but a great part of the paraphernalia of hostile procedure is absent. The judge sits down with the child who has been committed to the court, with members of the family, parole officers, and others who may help to make the situation comprehensible and indicates what steps can be taken to bring matters to a normal condition. We find the beginnings of scientific techniques in this study in the presence of the psychologist and medical officer who can report upon the mental and physical condition of the child, of the social workers who can report upon the situation of the families and neighborhood involved. Then there are other institutions beside the jails to which the children can be sent for prolonged observation and change of immediate environment. In centering interest upon reinstatement the sense of forward-looking moral responsibility is not only not weakened but is strengthened, for the court undertakes to determine what the child must do and be to take up normal social relations again. Where the responsibility rests upon others this can be brought out in much greater detail and with greater effect since it is not defined under abstract legal categories and the aim in determining responsibility is not to place punishment but to obtain future results. Out of this arises a much fuller presentation of the facts that are essential for dealing with the problem than can possibly appear in a criminal court procedure that aims to establish simply responsibility for a legally defined offense with the purpose of inflicting punishment. Of far greater importance is the appearance of the values of family relations, of schools, of training of all sorts, of opportunities to work, and of all the other factors that go to make up that which is worth while in the life of a child or an adult. Before the juvenile court it is possible to present all of these and all of them can enter the consideration of what action is to be taken. These are the things that are worthwhile. They are the ends that should determine conduct. It is impossible to discover their real import unless they can all be brought into relationship with each other.

It is impossible to deal with the problem of what the attitude and conduct of the community should be toward the individual who has broken its laws, or what his responsibility is in terms of future action, unless all the facts and all the values with reference to which the facts must be interpreted are there and can be impartially considered, just as it is impossible to deal scientifically with any problem without recognizing all the facts and all the values involved. The attitude of hostility which places the criminal under the ban, and thus takes him out of society, and prescribes a hostile procedure by which he is secured, tried, and punished can take into account only those features of his conduct which constitute infraction of the law, and can state the relation of the criminal and society only in the terms of trial for fixing guilt and of punishment. All else is irrelevant. The adult criminal court is not undertaking to readjust a broken-down social situation, but to determine by the application of fixed rules whether the man is a member of society in good and regular standing or is an outcast. In accordance with these fixed rules what does not come under the legal definition not only does not naturally appear but it is actually excluded. Thus there exists a field of facts bearing upon the social problems that come into our courts and governmental administrative bureaus, facts which cannot be brought into direct use in solving these problems. It is with this material that the social scientist and the voluntary social worker and his organizations are occupied. In the juvenile court we have a striking instance of this material forcing its way into the institution of the court itself and compelling such a change in method that the material can be actually used. Recent changes of attitude toward the family permit facts bearing upon the care of children which earlier lay outside the purview of the court to enter into its consideration.

Other illustrations could be cited of this change in the structure and function of institutions by the pressure of data which the earlier form of the institution had excluded. One may cite the earlier theory of charity that it was a virtue of those in fortunate circumstances which is exercised toward the poor whom we have always with us, in its contrast with the conception of organized charity whose aim is not the exercise of an individual virtue but such a change in the condition of the individual case and of the community within which the cases arise that a poverty which requires charity may disappear. The author of a medieval treatise on charity considering the lepers as a field for good works contemplated the possibility of their disappearance with the ejaculation "which may God forbid!" The juvenile court is but one instance of an institution in which the consideration of facts which had been regarded as irrelevant or exceptional has carried with it a radical change in the institution. But it is of particular interest because the court is the objective form of the attitude of hostility on the part of the community toward the one who transgresses its laws and customs, and it is of further interest because it throws into relief the two types of emotional attitudes which answer to two types of social organization. Over against the emotional solidarity of the group opposing the enemy we find the interests which spring up around the effort to meet and solve a social problem. These interests are at first in opposition to each other. The interest in the individual delinquent opposes the interest in property and the social order dependent upon it. The interest in the change of the conditions which foster the delinquent is opposed to that identified with our positions in society as now ordered, and the resentment at added responsibilities which had not been formerly recognized or accepted.

But the genuine effort to deal with the actual problem brings with it tentative reconstructions which awaken new interests and emotional values. Such are the interests in better housing conditions, in different and more adequate schooling, in playgrounds and small parks, in controlling child labor and in vocational guidance, in improved sanitation and hygiene, and in community and social centers. In the place of the emotional solidarity which makes us all one against the criminal there appears the cumulation of varied interests unconnected in the past which not only bring new meaning to the delinquent but which also bring the sense of growth, development, and achievement. This reconstructive attitude offers the cumulative interest which comes with interlocking diversified values. The discovery that tuberculosis, alcoholism, unemployment, school retardation, adolescent delinquency, among other social evils, reach their highest percentages in the same areas not only awakens the interest we have in combatting each of these evils, but creates a definite object, that of human misery, which focuses endeavor and builds up a concrete object of human welfare which is a complex of values. Such an organization of effort gives rise to an individual or self with a new content of character, a self that is effective since the impulses which lead to conduct are organized with reference to a clearly defined object.

It is of interest to compare this self with that which responds to the community call for defense of itself or its institutions. The dominant emotional coloring of the latter is found in the standing together of all the group against the common enemy. The consciousness which one has of others is stripped of the instinctive oppositions which in varying forms are aroused in us by the mere presence of others. These may be merely the slight rivalries and differences of opinion and of social attitude and position, or just the reserves which we all preserve over against those about us. In the common cause these can disappear. Their disappearance means a removal of resistance and friction and adds exhilaration and enthusiasm to the expression of one of the most powerful of human impulses. The result is a certain enlargement of the self in which one seems to be at one with everyone else in the group. It is not a self-consciousness in the way of contrasting one's self with others. One loses himself in the whole group in some sense, and may attain the attitude in which he undergoes suffering and death for the common cause. In fact just as war removes the inhibitions from the attitude of hostility so it quickens and commends the attitude of self-assertion of a self which is fused with all the others in the community. The ban upon self-assertion which the consciousness of others in the group to which one belongs carries with it disappears when the assertion is directed against an object of common hostility or dislike. Even in times of peace we feel as a rule little if any disapproval of arrogance toward those of another nationality, and national self-conceit and the denigration of the achievements of other peoples may become virtues. The same tendency exists in varying degree among those who unite against the criminal or against the party foe. Attitudes of difference and opposition between members of the community or group are in abeyance and there is given the greater freedom for self-assertion against the enemy. Through these experiences come the powerful emotions which serve to evaluate for the time being what the whole community stands for in comparison with the interests of the individual who is opposed to the group. These experiences, however, serve only to set off against each other what the group stands for and the meager birthright of the individual who cuts himself off from the group.

What we all fight for, what we all protect, what we all affirm against the detractor, confers upon each in some measure the heritage of all, while to be outside the community is to be an Esau without heritage and with every man's hand against him. Self-assertion against the common enemy, suppressing as it does the oppositions of individuals within the group and thus identifying them all in a common effort, is after all the self-assertion of the fight in which the opposing selves strive each to eliminate the other, and in so doing are setting up their own survival and the destruction of the others as the end. I know that many ideals have been the ends of war, at least in the minds of many of the fighters; that in so far the fighting was not to destroy the fighters but some pernicious institution, such as slavery, that many have fought bloody wars for liberty and freedom. No champions, however, of such causes have ever failed to identify the causes in the struggle with themselves. The battle is for the survival of the right party and the death of the wrong. Over against the enemy we reach the ultimate form of self-assertion, whether it is the patriotic national self, or the party, or the schismatic self, or the institutional self, or simply the self of the hand to hand mêlée. It is the self whose existence calls for the destruction, or defeat, or subjection, or reduction of the enemy. It is a self that finds expression in vivid, concentrated activity and under appropriate conditions of the most violent type. The instinct of hostility which provides the structure for this self when fully aroused and put in competition with the other powerful human complexes of conduct, those of sex, of hunger, and of parenthood and of possession has proved itself as more dominant than they. It also carries with it the stimulus for readier and, for the time being, more complete socialization than any other instinctive organization. There is no ground upon which men get together so readily as that of a common enemy, while a common object of the instinct of sex, of possession, or of hunger leads to instant opposition, and even the common object of the parental instinct may be the spring of jealousy. The socializing agency of common hostility is marked, as I have above indicated, by its own defects. In so far as it is the dominant instinct it does not organize the other instincts for its object. It suppresses or holds the others in abeyance. While hostility itself may be a constituent part of the execution of any instinct, for they all involve oppositions, there is no other instinctive act of the human self which is a constituent part of the immediate instinctive process of fighting, while struggle with a possible opponent plays its part in the carrying out of every other instinctive activity. As a result those who fight together against common enemies instinctively tend to ignore the other social activities within which oppositions between the individuals engaged normally arise.

It is this temporary relief from the social frictions which attend upon all other co-operative activities which is largely responsible for the emotional upheavals of patriotism, of mob consciousness, and the extremes of party warfare, as well as for the gusto of malicious gossiping and scandalmongering. Furthermore, in the exercise of this instinct success implies the triumph of the self over the enemy. The achievement of the process is the defeat of certain persons and the victory of others. The end takes the form of that sense of self-enlargement and assurance which comes with superiority of the self over others. The attention is directed toward the relative position of the self toward others. The values involved are those that only can be expressed in terms of interests and relations of the self in its differences from others. From the standpoint of one set of antagonists their victory is that of efficient civilization while the other regards their victory as that of liberal ideas. All the way from the Tamerlanes who create a desert and call it peace to the idealistic warriors who fight and die for ideas, victory means the survival of one set of personalities and the elimination of others, and the ideas and ideals that become issues in the contest must perforce be personified if they are to appear in the struggles that arise out of the hostile instinct. War, whether it is physical, economic, or political, contemplates the elimination of the physical, economic, or political opponent. It is possible to confine the operation of this instinct within certain specific limitations and fields. In the prize fights as in the olden tourneys the annihilation of the enemy is ceremonially halted at a fixed stage in the struggle. In a football game the defeated team leaves the field to the champion. Successful competition in its sharpest form eliminates its competitor. The victor at the polls drives the opponent from the field of political administration. If the struggle can be à *outrance* within any field and contemplates the removal of the enemy from that field, the instinct of hostility has this power of uniting and fusing the contesting groups, but since victory is the aim of the fight and it is the victory of one party over the other, the issues of battle must be conceived in terms of the victor and the vanquished.

Other types of social organization growing out of the other instincts, such as possession, hunger, or parenthood, imply ends which are not as such identified with selves in their oppositions to other selves, though the objects toward which these instinctive activities are directed may be occasion for the exercise of the hostile instinct. The social organizations which arise about these objects are in good part due to the inhibitions placed upon the hostile impulse, inhibitions which are exercised by the other groups of impulses which the same situations call out. The possession by one individual in a family or clan group of a desirable object is an occasion for an attack on the part of other members of the group, but his characters as a member of the group are stimuli to family and clan responses which check the attack. It may be mere repression with smoldering antagonisms, or there may be such a social reorganization that the hostility can be given a function under social control, as in the party, political, and economic contests, in which certain party, political, and economic selves are driven from the field leaving others that carry out the social activity. Here the contest being restricted the most serious evils of the warfare are removed, while the contest has at least the value of the rough selection. The contest is regarded in some degree from the standpoint of the social function, not simply from that of the elimination of an enemy. As the field of constructive social activity widens the operation of the hostile impulse in its instinctive form decreases. This does not, however, mean that the reactions that go to make up the impulse or instinct have ceased to function. It does mean that the impulse ceases to be an undertaking to get rid of the offending object by injury and destruction, that is, an undertaking directed against another social being with capacities for suffering and death—physical, economical, or political—like his own. It becomes in its organization with other impulses an undertaking to deal with a situation by removing obstacles. We still speak of him as fighting against his difficulties. The force of the original impulse is not lost but its objective is no longer the elimination of a person, but such a reconstruction that the profounder social activities may find their continued and fuller expression. The energy that expressed itself in burning witches as the causes of plagues expends itself at present in medical research and sanitary regulations and may still be called a fight with disease.

In all these changes the interest shifts from the enemy to the reconstruction of social conditions. The self-assertion of the soldier and conqueror becomes that of the competitor in industry or business or politics, of the reformer, the administrator, of the physician or other social functionary. The test of success of this self lies in the change and construction of the social conditions which make the self possible, not in the conquest and elimination of other selves. His emotions are not those of mass consciousness dependent upon suppressed individualities, but arise out of the cumulative interests of varied undertakings converging upon a common problem of social reconstruction. This individual and his social organization are more difficult of accomplishment and subject to vastly greater friction than those which spring out of war. Their emotional content may not be so vivid, but they are the only remedy for war, and they meet the challenge which the continued existence of war in human society has thrown down to human intelligence.

15

The Psychological Bases of
Internationalism*

THE WAR IN EUROPE has paid certain great spiritual dividends.
From Germany, from France, from England, and from Russia
have come accounts of the fusing of people and peoples into self
conscious nations. Men and women and children passed under the spell
of the great experience. They felt, if they did not think it out, that these
overwhelming moments of emotion were theirs because of their complete identification with each other in the whole community. It was
only because of this flood-tide of national consciousness that they could
be swept up to these ultimate heights of human experience. It was not
so much that they were willing to sacrifice themselves for their country,
as that for the time being they lived up to the enlargement of self-
consciousness which is the inner side of the consciousness of a nation.

The most impressive accounts of these experiences come not so
much from the outbursts of great masses in the cities, as from the letters
and reported incidents in the lives of families and individuals scattered
throughout these countries.

Now, these are types of the highest experiences that human nature
has attained. They are the same in nature with those of saints and
martyrs, and while they persist in full emotional throb, they make
possible what men and women have regarded as the greatest moments
in their lives. From the standpoint of the observer, the man may be
sacrificing himself for others; from his own, he is realizing the meaning
of his identity with his whole group.

* As originally published in *Survey*, XXXIII (1914–1915), 604–607.

We cannot remain long on these emotional heights. Devotion passes quite naturally into hatred of the enemy. This attitude, in the presence of actual danger to oneself and to all that has been precious, can be kept vivid and effective much longer than devotion. It is part of the almost instinctive technique of the community and the government to stimulate and play upon this hatred because it provides another mechanism for the sense of social identity after the exalted feeling of devotion has ebbed.

It does not necessarily detract from the lofty quality of the experiences that there was nothing in the attitudes of the peoples of Europe toward each other to account for the war itself.

There was, to be sure, among the people of France, Russia, and England, a sense of dread of the military power of Germany; and in Germany there was a widespread dread of the military power of Russia and France threatening Germany on both flanks, and of England upon the sea. But the actual populations of these different countries carried on without clash or hatred an international life of commerce, industry, and intellectual interchange in social ideas in literature, science, education, and even sport, which was beyond comparison more vivid and intimate than the national life in any country of Europe one hundred years ago. There never has been, within a shorter period than a century, so highly organized an intra-national life and consciousness in any country of the western world as the international life of Europe before the first of last August. There was, of course, one exception to this statement. Between the Serbs and Austrians existed a racial hatred of long standing that in Austria-Hungary, at least, called loudly for war.

With this exception, there was nothing in the minds of the peoples, in their attitudes toward each other, or in profound popular movements, that demanded or suggested war. Slavs in hundreds of thousands came every year into Germany to labor, not only in the harvest fields but even in manufacturing industry. The steady friendly invasion of France and England by Germans, took place without racial friction. The movement which was most profoundly popular, the labor movement, was international. Science was international. There was hardly a field of interest, within which there did not exist some international organization defining and asserting international standards.

There was not a social issue, an idea dear to the hearts of the European community, that could by any possibility be identified with any one nation or its peculiar institutions. There was far greater unanimity of the masses of the whole European population against the economic and social domination of the upper groups than of the mass of any nation against another people. In fact, with the exception of the

Austrian government in its attack upon Servia, no government has dared present to its people any issue except that of self-defense; and the whole effort of the publicity department of every chancellery among the powers at war, has been to present a case at home and abroad of a nation or a group of nations attacked without warrant and defending itself against unjustified aggression.

It would require the satire of a Swift or a Voltaire to do justice to the present situation, in which the greatest powers in Europe are engaged in the most terrible struggle the world has ever seen, while each is professedly occupied merely in self-defense. There is, of course, abundant reason for this identical formulation of the causes of the war. It is first of all an appeal to a public sentiment that is to be voiced by neutral nations; but, in the life and death grapple that is on, it is still more a mobilization of the moral forces at home. Nor are these two purposes distinct. Nations, like individuals, can become objects to themselves only as they see themselves through the eyes of others. Every appeal to public sentiment is an effort to justify oneself to oneself.

I doubt if we have fully realized the importance of this identical formulation of the causes of the war. Whatever else it means, it indicates clearly that for the masses of the European communities there is no justifiable cause of war except self-defense. There has arisen among the militaristic groups a revival of the cult of Napoleon with the appeal to the glory of combat and triumph. But not a military leader in Europe dares voice this appeal to slaughter and conquest.

Out of the warlike birth of the modern Prussian state and the German Empire under its hegemony, there has arisen a cult of the strong-armed state that finds justification for warfare in its own fortunes and in its own morale. But today there is not a German who can catch the public ear, who will recognize that the cult of Treitschke and von Bernhardi has an echo in the German nation. Throughout the western world there is now but one cause of war which can give rise to that entire national unity that constitutes the moral fitness for a life and death struggle—and that is, self-defense.

Unfortunately the theory of warfare demands offense as the most effective form of defense, and the logic of offense carries with it capture and subjection, devastation and terror. To defend successfully their own, men must get down to the primitive instincts from which spring battle-fury, the lust of carnage, rape, and rapine. But whatever may be said in justification of such offense from the standpoint of the sadistic psychologist, or of the Nietzschean counsel "to live dangerously," it is impossible to organize the moral sentiment of the fighting nations for a campaign of offensive warfare, and each government feels the compulsion upon it to suppress reports of that terror which is the logic of offensive fighting. An accepted and avowed policy of terrorism would be more dangerous to the administration at home than to the conquered people. And this is true not because a womanish sympathy has weakened the fiber of the peoples, but because the sense of social solidarity inevitably sweeps in the very people who are to be terrorized. The international fabric of European life could not be tossed aside when war was declared. Purely national cultures could not be substituted for the international culture of the western world, and no more convincing evidence of this could be given than the attempt which certain German scientists made in their letters to their American colleagues to prove that English science was entirely negligible. It was psychologically impossible for these men to hate the English as enemies of the fatherland as they wish to hate them, and still be on terms of international amity and co-operation within the field even of abstract science.

There is but one justification for killing which nations or individuals are willing to consciously accept, that of self-defense. The function of social organization is to build up and enlarge the personality of nations as truly as that of individuals, and this cannot include the deliberate destruction of the very members of international society, the consciousness of whom is essential to national self-consciousness.

But while it is true that it is psychologically impossible to mobilize a modern western nation for any but a defensive war, we cannot push aside the fact that these nations have been willing to accept military preparedness as an essential part of their national lives. The knowledge that the nation is prepared to fight has given it the feeling of self-respect that the knowledge of the art of self-defense and physical fitness give to the well-mannered man.

There has been a great deal of superficial justification of this military preparation for self-defense. Up to the first of last August, men could still maintain that preparation for war is the best guaranty of peace. Prince Kropotkin was the first to recognize publicly that the events which followed that date finally and utterly disproved this doctrine.

It has been stated that a nation in arms will not lightly go to war, and the phrase "a nation in arms" has been so pleasant on the tongue that men have stopped thinking when they have uttered it. A nation under arms is in fact a nation bound to the unthinking obedience of the soldier to his commander. It is not and cannot be a nation in conscious control of its own policies and its own fortunes. Could there be better evidence of this than the fact of the five great nations fighting with each other for national existence, while the people of all five believe that the war is one purely of self-defense? The government of each has assured them that this is the case.

"Theirs not to reason why;
Theirs but to do and die."

It is further maintained that in the relations of nations with each other, military power and readiness inspires international respect and enables a nation to enforce its rights without the final proof of the battlefield. In the words of our own militarist, a nation with the big stick may speak softly. And here again the picture is so agreeable that we are loath to look to the history of diplomacy. There it stands very plainly written that as soon as military force is admitted into the argument, it as inevitably crowds out considerations of right, as a file of soldiers introduced into a convention or a court silences every claim except that supported by the bayonet.

Lord Grey stretched his diplomat's imagination nearly to the breaking point when he conceived of England as approaching Germany's situation from the standpoint of national right as distinct from national might, and appealed to the seemingly unrealizable ideal formulated by Gladstone, of a public right governing European nations.

We have been living largely in diplomatic papers, and have sat with statesmen and monarchs agonizing over the terror that they foresaw and could not forefend even when they hesitatingly suggested the impossible, an international right, that might conceivably be put into the scales over against orders of mobilizations and dates and provisions of ultimata. The monstrous puerility of it all!

Because of the pomp and circumstance of diplomatic intercourse, and the terrible consequences it implies, we overlook the fact that there is at present no situation short of a street fight or a small boys' squabble in which the actual procedure is the same as that of our ministers plenipotentiary and ambassadors extraordinary. And there is but one explanation: When there is an armed force behind every proposal, the only convincing counter argument is a *force majeure*; and when this argument has been displayed, any other is a work of supererogation. There is but one possible justification for the situation, and it is the one offered—the necessity of it.

"There is no international right that anyone needs to respect. Between nations, except in moments of exaltation, might is the only right."

While we are reading governmental papers we may accept it. We are back in the age of the Hohenstaufens, when the only guardian of international rights was the Lord of Hosts, the God of Battles.

The curious thing is that while we agree with the diplomatist and

155

the war lord behind him that there is no international right, we would have sent any man not a diplomat to an insane asylum who acted upon that theory. A Frenchman or Englishman who made a contract with a German and refused to keep it, an Italian scientist who laid claim to the achievements of a Russian physiologist, an Englishman who outraged a Belgian peasant girl, on the theory that there was no international right, would all have realized, not only in the country in which the offense was committed, but also in their own countries, that there is an international right that is quite indistinguishable from national right.

In any case, the fellow-countrymen of that grandson of a Scotchman who was born in Koenigsberg, Germany, and who is so loudly acclaimed by that Teutonized Englishman, Houston Chamberlain—the fellow-countrymen of Immanuel Kant, at least, might recognize that the only reason there is any right at all in any nation or country is because there is a right that is recognized as international and more than international.

We know from some expensive experience that there is no such thing as national finance that is not founded upon international finance. We know there never has been a national science that has not been the outgrowth of an international science. We know not only that there never has been a civilized race that is not a mingling of many bloods, but that no self-conscious civilization has ever arisen except out of the intercourse of ideas which have been actually internationalized and have thus become universal. A standard of any sort could not be merely national unless it were willing to be a contradiction in terms.

In a word, no nation could come to consciousness as a nation except within an international society, and there is no capacity or right or achievement of any nation for which it is not as dependent upon the international society that has made the nation possible, as is any German or Englishman or Russian dependent upon his own society for his capacities and rights and achievements.

Now it is true that human rights, being social growths, have been slow growths, and that their growth has been marked by the same sort of violence as that which now on a Brobdignagian scale is devastating Europe. It is, then, easy to assume that international right is a plant of still slower growth, and that we must have the divine patience for which a thousand years is as one day, and one day is as a thousand years. We must assume, according to this doctrine, that when our war lords and foreign secretaries and militaristic leaders address us we are still in the age of the Hohenstaufens and their shining armors, while words addressed to the world by the Pasteurs, the Kochs, the Mendelieffs, the

Ibsens, the Anatole Frances, the Darwins, the Sir Henry Maines, the great industrialists, educators, and financiers reach their fellow-country-men because a twentieth century international society gave them both their social equipment and their equally essential audience.

We know the doctrine is a false one. We know that we have not only all the mechanisms necessary for expressing international rights of which we are vividly conscious, but also for enforcing them. We know that it is only the unwillingness of the peoples of our so-called Christendom to surrender that peculiar egoistic consciousness which each one of us experiences when his own nation stands up and shakes its fist in the face of another nation, together with the more profound experiences of self-devotion which go with it, that has kept Europe from working out and presenting for enactment international legislation that at a stroke would have replaced nations submissively bowing before their under officers and drill sergeants, and quite at the mercy of their foreign offices, by a Hague or other tribunal and a small international police.

We know that it is not because the rights of people and peoples can be affirmed and protected only by the procedure of the Hohenstaufens or the more modern street ruffians, that we have refused to permit international institutions to formulate those rights and an international public opinion to enforce them.

What we are afraid to lose is this peculiar national self-consciousness, the sense of superiority to people of other nations, and the patriotism and lofty devotion which seems to be dependent upon national egotisms. We will not surrender these nor the occasions out of which they arise. There must be some things we are unwilling to arbitrate, otherwise we are craven people with dead souls.

It is of importance that men should realize that the problem of war is on the one hand ethical and on the other, psychological. It is not a problem of institutional mechanisms, nor of an apparatus of universal ideas, nor of means of international communication and acquaintanceship. It is not a question, in other words, of creating an international society. All of these exist. It is a question of relative values. Are the spiritual experiences, both the egotistical and those of self-surrender, both the contemptible and the heroic, which seem to us to pre-suppose war—are these so valuable that we can afford to purchase them at the expense of Armageddon?

The problem is an ethical problem because it is a conflict of values. The western world has now a definite bill of costs for its procedure in checking and cutting back the growth of the institutions and public sentiments which could without difficulty have settled the quarrel that was the occasion of Europe's holocaust. And on the other side, it has experienced the values for the sake of which it has exposed itself to this loss.

There have been those moments of priceless emotional experience, in which men and women realized that they were all one when the nation was in danger. With many, this elevated emotional tone will continue. With most, it has ebbed into the compelling routine of the group of habits we call discipline; in very many, into the hatred of the enemy by which one can still get that sense of solidarity that under other conditions we call mob consciousness.

These are enormously valuable experiences—even those which must be called ignoble in comparison with the sense of entire self-devotion. They pervade the whole consciousness, giving even insignificant objects and experiences a vicarious import. There have been periods in former struggles for human liberty when these moments stood out not only as worth while in themselves, but with the added value of the issues for which men were fighting. Today, men are fighting for no ideas. No nation is fighting for a better order of society. The international order of society is better than that of any nation which reserves to itself the right of fighting for any issue it chooses to call vital to its own interests.

This war has taken place because the nations have maintained the right to carry arms and thus have made a relatively insignificant incident the occasion for a European catastrophe.

It is of importance that the relative values should stand out clearly. It is probable that in the aftermath of the war, these values will come with ever greater definiteness to men's minds. Unless men are so circumstanced that they cannot reflect, they must gradually recognize that as nations—apart from small interested groups—they were fighting simply because they demanded as their highest privilege the right to fight on any occasion, and at any time.

It is an ethical question, then, because, perhaps for the first time in human history, the value of war as a social institution existing for its own exercise, for its use in social organization, in physical training, in heightened national self-feeling, in opportunities for limitless hatreds and self-devotions, has been put sharply in contrast with the costs and losses of warfare.

It is a psychological question because the values of war, and the preparation for it, have to be stated more and more completely in terms of attitudes and states of mind. The objective human interests for which men have fought in the past are now so embodied in the institutions of civilized states, and in the habits and customs of communities that they are there vastly better safeguarded than they could be by armies and navies. It is the feeling of enlarged personality, of the national *amour propre,* a feeling not so much of what a people have or want as of what they are, that militarism supports in national life.

If the ethical problem arises out of the conflict between values which a national military attitude and training maintains and those which war destroys, the psychological question is whether the military attitude and training are essential for the self-respect of a nation; whether this antiquated, medieval method of giving every man the sense of being at one with the rest of the community must be preserved for the lack of better mechanism.

If the ethical problem is solved as we hope that it will be solved, if militarism is cashiered because it is too hideously expensive in human values, the question as to the way in which nations will arouse their patriotisms is likely to be left to answer itself. But though men are not likely to consider what form patriotisms will take in the future, it is true that because the problem has become so largely psychological, the ethical problem of war stands out so clearly.

It is because in the relations of western nations with each other we have nothing left to fight for except the right to fight for the sake of fighting, that we can squarely assess the value of this so-called national right. If bloodless revolution had not been embodied in the constitution of most of our western states, war would be still necessary to bring men to the common consciousness of their rights and their willingness to die for them. At present, any war is apt to be more dangerous than helpful to interests of those in our communities who need protection. In these days of scientific warfare, the disciplined populace who make up the army become the bulwark of economic and social privilege. No. At present, war, as an institution, cannot be cast in the rôle of Greatheart who goes forth to protect the weak. It must find alone in the consciousness of fighting and being ready to fight, all the values with which to offset the losses it entails.

Instinctively all those who were interested in social reform felt that this war must set back the clock of social betterment unless it accomplished the feat of destroying militarism itself. And here the militarist stiffens the sinews, throws out his chest, and contrasts his red-blooded virility with the feminist, philanthropic social reform, and asks us whether we are willing to exchange the fighting man for the milksop.

We will not stop to consider the childish assumption that we must pull down amid fire and slaughter the whole structure of the western world to secure bulging sinews, deep chests, and red blood corpuscles. The real question is: Why should anyone consider the work with which these reforms are occupied as white-blooded and feministic? They are the identical interests—though vastly more intelligently conceived—for which our forefathers fought, bled, and died. They are attempted concrete definitions of the life, the liberty, and the pursuit of happiness of the great mass of the community. We cannot fight for them any longer, at least after the fashion of the modern fighting state, because the militaristic state must look upon itself as the potential enemy of all other states while most of the social structure within which growth is taking place is international. The state as the instrument of the separate community is the organ through which these changes get formulated in that nation. But as long as it is necessarily hostile to internationalism, it cannot become properly responsive to the labor movement, to social science, or even to industry. It follows that these movements of social reform and integration within the separate states are deformed, are allowed to advance only so far as the interests of the state in its separation permits them to go.

The result is that the so-called reformer is always on the begging hand over against the self-sufficient state. How far may the reform go without weakening the fixed order of society? There is certainly no process more definitely international than industry and commerce. But industry is divided up from the governmental standpoint into industries of the different nations, and barriers are set up to bring in a national net income by industries that are conceived of as if they could stand alone. There can be no adequate standard of social control of an essentially international industry, from the point of view of a national budget. *The reformer stands in the position of the man urging concessions in the interests of humanity, and at the expense of the state.*

Now, there are restricted fields, such as that of hygiene, in which national and international interest palpably coincide. Here the trained man speaks with authority and does not present a pathetic plea. Even here, of course, there are limits to state action.

The German militaristic state has, more intelligently than any other, recognized the common grounds of international social growth and national state interests. Within these fields militarism has even advanced these reforms. The German bureaucracy has gained a certain detachment from the military standpoint of its government, which has enabled it to introduce industrial insurance, community care for infants, the fostering of vocational education, and better housing among other reforms. The privileged interests, which have opposed these reforms in other countries have been summarily pushed to one side by a purposeful government that has undertaken to make its people more effective, more powerful, more masterful than any other nation in the world.

Such a state can have only persecution for an international labor movement, whereas it will welcome an international hygiene. It will welcome an international physical science which puts nature under the control of a national industry, whereas it will frown upon Hague tribunals which would deal with conflicts of nations from the international instead of the national standpoints.

Even in Germany the social reformer brings his program to a government that has other interests besides those of international society, and asks somewhat humbly how much of his program may be accepted. If science, and hygiene, and education, and art, and industry, and commerce, were as narrowly national as are armament and warfare in their interests, the social reformer would speak with authority and not as something of a milksop who is after all only trying to get a little good done.

Militarism is not simply an evil in itself. It is typical and conservative of a state that is narrowly national in its attitude and that refuses to recognize the international society, that after all has made the self-conscious state possible. The problem is then largely a psychological problem, for it has to do with the change of attitude, the willingness to accept the whole international fabric of society, and to regard the states and the communities of which they are the instruments, as subject to and controlled by the life of the whole, not as potential enemies for whose assault each state must be forever on the watch.